Corporate Transition

An Essential Guide for Academic Graduates

Sanath Nair

Chapter Content

Dedication

Dedicated to my loving wife and adventurous son, the lights of my life.

To my wife, who has brought endless joy and laughter into my life, I dedicate this book to you. Your unwavering love and support have been the foundation upon which I have built this work of my heart. Thank you for being my partner in all things, for your endless patience, and for making our home a warm and loving place.

To my son, who has added so much adventure and wonder to my world. Your boundless energy and zest for life inspire me to dream big and live boldly. I hope this book will encourage you to pursue your passions and embrace the beauty of the unknown.

Together, you are the wind beneath my wings, the driving force behind my every success, and the reason I have the courage to chase my dreams. This book is for you and I dedicate it with all my love.

Sanath Nair

Preface

Transitioning from academia to the corporate world can be a challenging experience, filled with uncertainty and anxiety. As a recent graduate or a final-year student, you may have questions about how to make the most of your newfound job and navigate the complex world of corporate policies, office politics, and career growth.

"Corporate Transition - An Essential Guide for Academic Graduates" is a comprehensive guidebook that provides readers with practical advice and real-life examples of how to navigate this transition successfully. With 15 chapters written from the perspective of four recent grads and their wise mentor, this book covers everything from acing interviews and understanding company policies to building relationships with colleagues and balancing work and personal life.

As a seasoned professional with years of experience in the corporate world, I've gathered valuable insights and strategies that can help you achieve professional growth without sacrificing your personal life. This book is filled with practical tips and advice that you can apply to your own life, but let me make one thing clear: there is no one-size-fits-all formula for success.

I've observed countless patterns and styles throughout my career, and I'm excited to share them with you. From managing your time effectively to developing your skills and building strong relationships, these tried-and-true methods will help you reach your goals and make progress in your career. But ultimately, success depends on your unique situation and personal drive.

Whether you are just starting your career in the corporate world or looking to make a change, this guidebook is an invaluable resource. It will equip you with all the tools necessary for success, from time management and productivity tips to preparing for the future and setting career goals.

I am proud to present this comprehensive resource to you. I hope that this guidebook will help you navigate your journey from academia to the corporate world with confidence and ease.

Sanath Nair

Prologue

It was a crisp autumn morning in Bengaluru, India, and the campus of the prestigious B-School was abuzz with excitement. The students had been eagerly awaiting this day for weeks, as they had heard the news that the famous CEO of a tech company based in London, Victor Edmund, was coming to deliver a lecture series. Victor was a well-known figure in the tech industry and was admired by all for his innovative ideas and bold leadership style. As the students made their way to the lecture hall, they could sense anticipation in the air. When they entered the hall, they were greeted by a large stage, adorned with flowers and a podium, on which the CEO would be speaking. They took their seats and looked around, eager to hear what the CEO had to say.

Suddenly, the lights in the hall dimmed and a spotlight shone on the stage. The students held their breaths as Victor Edmund walked onto the stage, his confident stride, and warm smile-inspiring the students. He greeted the students with a wave and began his lecture.

"Good morning, students. It's a great pleasure to be here today, sharing my life story and the lessons I've learned on my journey from college grad to successful CEO. Today, I want to talk about the transition from academia to the corporate world. It's a journey that can be both challenging and rewarding, but with the right preparation, it can also be one of the most fulfilling experiences of your life," said Victor.

Victor went on to explain what students can expect from his lecture series. He shared his opinion regarding the differences in culture, expectations, and work environment between the academic and corporate worlds. He spoke about the fast-paced and competitive nature of the corporate world, the need for quick decision-making, and the importance of adapting to change. He also spoke about the benefits of making the transition, such as the opportunity to apply what you've learned in real-world scenarios, the chance to make a significant impact, and the financial rewards that come with it.

"So, how can you prepare for this journey?" asked Victor. He then provided tips on how to make a smooth transition, including networking, building relationships, continuous learning, and personal growth.

Aarvi, Inaya, Druv, and Sameer, four students from the college, arrived for the lecture with enthusiasm and excitement. As the lecture was concluding, the four students were bursting with anticipation. They had a strong desire for greater knowledge and were determined to take the opportunity at hand. What they wanted was MORE. Deciding to take a chance, they walked up towards the CEO, fueled with motivation and drive. A burning need to make an impression on him propelled them as they journeyed up to seek greater insight into his perspective.

Victor was swept away by their view on life, almost surprised to see how lucky he was for having stumbled upon such bright individuals. Victor noticed that these eager students were genuinely keen on learning more, and he wasn't ready to discount their golden opportunity for growth. He found no cause or excuse for not offering what he knew the best, enlightening them with wise perspectives from the corporate world and possibilities in life. He recognized that the perfect mentoring session he had been hoping for was here and immediately extended an invitation for tea to those four shining faces.

Aarvi and Inaya were star-struck. Meanwhile, Druv and Sameer were overjoyed as they felt like they were floating on Clouds. Their mesmerizing feat captivated the CEO's attention and left them speechless. It was a moment to remember, what else could this mean for these four bright and talented young future entrepreneurs besides a personal audience with the top executives of one of the world's leading tech giants?

Little did anyone know that this conversation was soon going to lead to a lifelong mentorship over tea!

Introduction to the transition from the academic to the corporate world

As the sun set on the campus, Aarvi, Inaya, Druv, and Sameer went to the campus tea room to meet with Victor Edmund, the CEO of a successful tech company based in London. They were eager to learn from this successful businessman and hear about his journey from college grad to CEO.

When they arrived at the tea room, they found it bathed in a soft glow, creating an intimate atmosphere. Victor was already there, pouring them a steaming tea before settling in his seat. The students were on the edge of theirs, waiting for him to begin speaking.

"As you embark on your journey transitioning from academia to the corporate world," he began solemnly, "it's natural to feel equal parts excitement and uncertainty. You may have honed your skills and knowledge while studying and preparing for your future career. However, the corporate world is entirely different with its expectations and challenges."

He added, "One of the key differences between the academic and corporate world is how information is communicated. Writing lengthy reports or papers filled with technical jargon and intricate details is expected in the academic world. However, effective communication is often the key to success in the corporate world. Here, it's essential to convey information in a concise, direct manner that is easily understood by your colleagues and clients.

He provided an example: "Imagine you are working on a project for a client," he said, "and you need to provide an update to your team. This could involve creating a detailed document with complex technical language in academia. Yet, in the corporate world, this could be done through presenting clear points visually so everyone can understand."

Inaya and Sameer were full of questions, eager to know more. . Inaya asked, "What makes effective communication? How can one develop such skills? And how do I present myself professionally within this new environment?"

Victor's response was simple but profound, "Adapting your communication style to the corporate environment is just one of the many ways you'll need to adjust as you make the transition. But don't worry! With an open mind and a willingness to learn, you'll be able to thrive in your new role. Continuously seeking out opportunities for growth and development, such as attending workshops or courses, will also show your commitment to staying current and relevant industry trends and demonstrate your eagerness to continue growing your skills."

"The transition may be challenging, but with a focus on adapting to the expectations of your new environment, a commitment to continuous learning, and a drive to build strong relationships, you'll be well on your way to success. Embrace the new opportunities and challenges of this exciting new chapter. You'll find that the corporate world is where you can continue growing, learning, and succeeding," he said.

Inaya and Sameer sat across from the CEO, eagerly awaiting his wisdom. He slowly sipped his tea before leaning back in his chair and looking them both in the eyes.

He continued, "As you embark on the exciting journey of transitioning from the academic to the corporate world, the first step is understanding the unique culture and expectations of the business environment. The corporate world is based on a foundation of relationships, results, and performance. Success in this environment requires more than just knowledge and skills."

The CEO was happy to share his experiences and advice on how best to prepare for their transition into the corporate world. He started by emphasizing the importance of perception in the corporate world. "In this environment, perception is reality," he said, "and your professional and personal reputation will be paramount to success."

He added, "This means that you will be evaluated not only on your expertise and ability to get the job done but also on how you interact with others and professionally present yourself."

He gave another example to emphasize his statement, "For example, let's say you're working on a project with a tight deadline. In the academic world, you may have been able to rely solely on your knowledge and skills to complete the project. However, in the corporate world, the project's success may also depend on your ability to collaborate effectively with your team and communicate with stakeholders clearly and confidently. This underscores the importance of building strong relationships and maintaining a professional demeanor. These skills will be crucial to your projects and career success."

Aarvi and Druv listened intently, taking notes as the CEO spoke. They were interested in how they could prepare themselves for this transition.

"It's important to remember that building relationships takes time and effort, but the rewards are well worth it. A strong network of professional contacts can open doors and provide opportunities for growth and advancement. Your professional demeanor, including your communication style, attitude, and work ethic, will also contribute to your reputation and play a significant role in your success in the corporate world," advised the CEO.

The CEO addressed the students with a warm smile, "I understand that many of you are preparing to enter the corporate world, and I want to discuss what this transition may entail. It's important to remember that the corporate environment is unique in its own right. So your approach to it should be different. To excel in this new setting, you should focus on building strong relationships, keeping a professional attitude, and proactively searching for opportunities for growth and development. An open outlook, a thirst for knowledge, and a passion for success will bring wonderful results!!!"

One of the key differences between the academic and corporate worlds is how information is communicated. Communication is often more formal in the academic world, emphasizing technical language and academic jargon. However, the corporate world focuses on clear and concise communication, using plain language and avoiding technical terms unless necessary."

CEO Added, "Transitioning from one style of communication to the other can be challenging. But with practice and a commitment to continuous learning, you'll soon find that you can effectively communicate in both environments. Understanding the differences in communication styles is critical to your transition."

Victor gave another example to better understand Aarvi, Inaya, Druv, and Sameer.

"In a college presentation, you may have been used to using technical terms and academic jargon to impress your professors. However, in a corporate setting, using overly technical language can confuse your colleagues and make it difficult for them to understand your point. Instead, focus on using plain language and clearly stating your ideas concisely and directly. This will help ensure that your message is well received and that your ideas are given the consideration they deserve."

The students listened as the CEO continued, sharing his insights and experiences. They were grateful for the opportunity to learn from someone as successful and knowledgeable as Victor Edmund.

Aarvi and Druv were listening intently, taking notes as the CEO spoke. They were interested in how they could prepare themselves for this transition.

He continued....

"Effective communication is not just about getting your point across in the corporate world. It is also about building relationships and fostering collaboration. By adapting your communication style to the corporate environment and focusing on clear and concise language, you'll be able to communicate more effectively with your colleagues, stakeholders, and clients. This, in turn, will help you build stronger relationships and contribute to your overall success in the corporate world."

Victor Edmund addressed a group of four bright young minds completing their college degrees soon. Aarvi, Inaya, Druv, and Sameer were all eager to learn what the transition from the academic to the corporate world would be like. Victor calmly explained that communication styles had to be adapted to communicate effectively in both environments.

He reminded them, "As you transition from the academic to the corporate world, it's important to understand the differences in communication styles and to develop the skills necessary to communicate effectively in both environments. With practice and a commitment to continuous learning, you'll soon be able to communicate in a way that is both effective and engaging. You'll be well on your way to a successful and fulfilling career in the corporate world."

Aarvi was particularly interested in this topic and asked for more information on developing her network.

Victor suggested, "Networking is a critical component of success in the corporate world, as it allows you to build relationships with your colleagues and expand your reach within the industry. Expanding your network allows you to create opportunities, stay informed about industry trends and advancements, and gain a wider perspective on the corporate world."

He added, "Attending industry events, joining professional organizations, and actively seeking opportunities to connect with others in your field is essential to developing your professional network. For example, attending a conference related to your industry can be an excellent opportunity to connect with others in your field and build new relationships. You never know who you might meet at these events. You may come across someone who works at a company you admire. By building a relationship with them, you can tap into their network and potentially open doors to new opportunities."

The group discussed this advice further over cups of tea, coming up with ideas of who to reach out to make new connections. They made a pact to commit to expanding their networks as best they could, no matter how daunting the task seemed at first glance.

The CEO emphasized, "In the corporate world, relationships are everything. The more people you know, the more opportunities you will have. The key to success in Networking is to be authentic, build real relationships, and stay in touch with your contacts over time. Doing so will create a valuable network of professionals who can help you navigate the corporate world and achieve your career goals."

"Networking is not just about meeting new people. It's about building genuine and meaningful relationships with those in your industry. You can build a strong professional network that will support you throughout your career by actively seeking opportunities to connect with others and engaging in meaningful conversations. For example, let's say you attend a networking event and meet someone who works in a similar field. After chatting for a few minutes, you discover that you share a common interest in a certain aspect of your industry. You exchange business cards and agree to meet for coffee to discuss the topic further. This one meeting could lead to a valuable mentorship opportunity, a referral to a potential job opportunity, or even a lifelong friendship in the industry. The opportunities are endless, but it all starts with taking the first step and actively building your professional network." He added.

Aarvi, Inaya, Druv, and Sameer had started attending Victor's workshop on transitioning from the academic world to the corporate one. They had been inspired by their CEO, Victor Edmund's words of wisdom "In the fast-paced corporate world, it is essential to stay ahead of the game by constantly expanding your knowledge and skills. By being open to learning and growth, you position yourself for success and set yourself apart from your peers."
aarvi

Aarvi shared her thoughts first. "For example, I'm in the marketing department at my company. If I noticed a shift in consumer behavior towards sustainable products, I would take it upon myself to research and learn more about this trend to come up with fresh ideas for my team," she said. "By doing this, I demonstrate my commitment to my career and my versatility and adaptability, which will be highly recognized in any company," she concluded... "It's important to never stop learning because the more you invest in yourself, the more you reap its benefits."

Victor was delighted with Aarvi's thoughts. He said, "For instance, imagine you work in the marketing department of a tech company and read about the growing trend of using augmented reality in advertising. Instead of ignoring it, you dive deeper into this area and attend a workshop on AR marketing. You better understand the technology and its applications, network with field experts, and bring new ideas back to your company. This showcases your initiative and drives to stay ahead of the curve and bring value to your company. Your willingness to learn and grow sets you apart as a driven and proactive professional and can lead to increased responsibilities and opportunities for growth within the company."

It was getting dark outside. Aarvi, Inaya, Druv, and Sameer had to return to their hostels.

Finally, Victor concluded, "Moving from the academic to the corporate world can be an exciting yet intimidating journey. But with the right mindset, attitude, and approach, you can make a smooth transition and succeed professionally. By recognizing the differences in culture, communication styles, and expectations, and by focusing on developing your professional network, learning, growing, and building relationships, you can lay the foundation for a successful and fulfilling career in the corporate world."

As the evening ended, the CEO stood up and shook hands with each student. "Remember, the transition from academia to the corporate world is not easy, but it is a rewarding experience if you are prepared and willing to put in the effort," he said with a smile.

The students left the tea room feeling inspired and motivated, eager to start their journey to success. They knew that the lessons they were about to learn would stay with them for the rest of their lives.
Walking back to their hostels, four friends discussed how they could apply this knowledge as they passed through the hostel gate.

Sameer thoughtfully concluded as they reached their hostels, "It's true that if we make an effort now, it will pay off later. So let's dedicate ourselves to embracing new opportunities for learning and growing to stand out from our peers!"

With renewed enthusiasm, all four friends headed off towards their rooms after wishing each other good luck for their assignments coming up for tomorrow.

Understanding Corporate Culture and Expectations

The next day, the students woke up early, eager to attend the CEO's lecture. They went to the campus lecture hall, where Victor Edmund awaited them. As the students took their seats and the CEO approached the stage, the room was excitedly buzzing.

"Good morning, everyone," the CEO started. "Today, we will discuss the importance of understanding corporate culture and expectations."

The students sat up straight, paying close attention to the CEO's words.

As the lecture began, Victor grabbed the students' attention by giving real-life examples of companies that failed due to a lack of understanding of their corporate culture. He explained how a company's culture sets the tone for how employees interact with each other and how they approach their work.

"A company's culture is like its DNA," he said. "It defines its values, beliefs, and the way it operates. It is crucial for employees, especially those in leadership positions, to understand and embrace their company's culture."

The students were enthralled by Victor's words and listened intently. He explained how a company's expectations also play a crucial role in determining its success. "Expectations are the unwritten rules that dictate how employees should behave and perform," he said. "If expectations are not communicated clearly, employees can become confused and demotivated, negatively impacting the company."

After the lecture, Victor waved to Aarvi, Druv, Inaya, and Sameer and signaled them to meet him in the cafeteria at 5 pm. The four students were thrilled. They couldn't wait to have a chat with him.

The four students, Aarvi, Druv, Inaya, and Sameer, arrived at the cafeteria with excitement and nervousness. They had heard so much about CEO Victor Edmund and couldn't believe they were about to converse with him.

As they approached his table, Victor welcomed them with a warm smile. "Hello, students. Please, have a seat," he said.

The students took their seats one by one. Victor smiled and, adjusting his overcoat, asked them about their interests and careers. Aarvi, who was interested in marketing, spoke about her passion for creating campaigns that connect with people on an emotional level. Druv, interested in finance, discussed his goal of becoming a financial analyst for a prominent investment firm.

Inaya, who was interested in human resources, spoke about improving workplace culture and employee satisfaction. And Sameer, who was interested in technology, talked about his dream of starting his own tech company.

Victor listened to each student with genuine interest and offered them valuable advice and insights. "Aarvi, your passion for connecting with people makes a great marketer," he said. "Druv, you have a keen eye for finance, and you can reach your goal with hard work and determination. Inaya, improving workplace culture is crucial for the success of any company. And Sameer, starting your own tech company takes a lot of courage and vision. I have no doubt you'll achieve your dream."

The students were impressed by how approachable, and down-to-earth Victor was. He made them feel heard and valued, and they appreciated his honest and straightforward advice.

Victor shared his experiences and insights about the corporate world as the conversation continued. He talked about his challenges, how he overcame them, and the lessons he learned along the way. The students were fascinated by his stories and asked him many questions.

Victor continued, "When you enter the corporate world, it is crucial to understand the company's mission and values, as well as the norms and unwritten workplace rules. This will help you fit in and succeed in your role."

Druv nodded, taking notes. "What about the company's mission and values?" he asked.

"The company's mission and values are the guiding principles that drive the company's decisions and actions. It is important to understand these principles to align your actions with the company's goals and values. This will help you fit in and give you a sense of purpose and motivation in your role," the CEO explained.

Aarvi raised her hand next. "How do we learn about the company's culture and expectations?" she asked.

"The best way to learn about the company's culture and expectations is to research. Read about the company online, talk to current and former employees, and ask about the company culture during the interview process. This will give you a good idea of what to expect and help you prepare for the transition," the CEO said.

Sameer leaned forward, eager to ask the next question. "What if we find out that the company's culture is not a good fit for us?" he asked.

The CEO smiled. "That's a good question. Suppose the company's culture is not a good fit for you. In that case, having an open and honest conversation with your manager is important. If the differences are too great, it may be better to find a company that is a better fit for your values and work style."

The students sat silently, digesting all the information the CEO had shared.

Victor saw a bit confused state in all of them. He said calmly, "Let me explain these concepts in detail."

He added, "Starting a new job can be exciting, full of new opportunities and a chance to make a difference. However, it is important to approach this transition cautiously, as the company culture and expectations can play a crucial role in your success in the workplace. To ensure that you are aligned with the company's mission and values, it is essential to understand what is expected of you and how the company operates."

"Corporate culture is the collective personality of an organization and is shaped by its history, people, and leadership style. It encompasses the company's shared beliefs, values, behaviors, and customs, from its mission and vision to how employees interact with each other and the outside world. It is critical to comprehend a company's mission and values to comprehend its culture. These should be reflected in the company's operations, policies, and practices and can help guide you as you navigate your new role."

"For example, if a company strongly emphasizes work-life balance, they likely offer flexible schedules and remote work options and encourage employees to take time off when needed. On the other hand, if a company prioritizes productivity and efficiency, it may have strict deadlines and a fast-paced work environment. By understanding the company's mission and values, you can ensure that your values and goals align with those of the organization."

He desired the student to learn better. "Company culture is crucial to success in any organization," Victor added. It includes a company's shared views, values, habits, and customs. It plays a significant role in shaping the workplace environment. Understanding a company's corporate culture and expectations is essential for new employees to thrive and achieve success."

Victor leaned on his chair, took the cup, and sipped some tea. He said, "Corporate culture is critical to success in any workplace. It encompasses an organization's shared beliefs, values, behaviors, and customs. It plays a significant role in shaping the workplace environment. Understanding a company's corporate culture and expectations is essential for new employees to thrive and achieve success."

"In addition to the formal mission and values, the unwritten rules and norms within a workplace can significantly impact an employee's success. For example, consider a company that values open communication and collaboration. In this scenario, it may be expected that employees regularly attend team meetings, contribute to group discussions, and offer constructive feedback. On the other hand, a company that values privacy and individual achievement may expect employees to work independently and avoid discussing confidential information with others."

Inaya raised her hand, eager to know more. "Can you give us examples of what you mean by norms and unwritten rules?" she asked.

The CEO smiled. "Of course. For example, some companies have a more relaxed dress code, while others have a more formal one. Some companies encourage open communication, while others have a more hierarchical structure. It is important to understand these nuances so that you can be successful in your role."

"Observing the behavior and attitudes of colleagues is one way to get a sense of a company's culture and expectations. For instance, in a company that values punctuality, you may notice that all employees arrive at the office on time and take their lunch breaks at the designated time. On the other hand, in a company that values flexibility, you may observe that employees can work from home or set their schedules. Paying attention to these cues can help you understand what is acceptable and not."

He stood up, approached Aarvi, and looked straight into her eyes. He continued, "Asking questions is another effective way to gain insight into a company's culture and expectations. For example, you could ask your supervisor or colleagues about the company's preferred communication style or the standard working hours. Asking these questions shows that you are interested in the company and committed to aligning your behavior and attitudes with those of the organization."

Addressing all students, Victor added, "In conclusion, understanding a workplace's unwritten rules and norms is just as important as understanding the formal mission and values. Observing your colleagues, asking questions, and paying attention to the company's expectations can help you thrive in your new role and align with the company's culture and goals. An example of the necessity of understanding corporate culture and expectations is the story of an employee who joined a company that prioritizes punctuality, only to discover that the company has a permissive approach to timekeeping. The employee was consistently late for meetings and took longer lunch breaks, which was not in line with the company's expectations and negatively impacted their performance. By understanding the company's culture and expectations, the employee could have adjusted their behavior to align with its values and achieve success."

"One thing I've learned is that success is not just about achieving your goals but also about enjoying the journey," said Victor. "Find a career you're passionate about, and the rest will follow. And always surround yourself with people who support and encourage you."

As the conversation ended, the students thanked Victor for his time and valuable advice. They left the cafeteria feeling inspired and motivated and with a newfound respect for the CEO.

"I can't believe we just had a conversation with the CEO," said Aarvi, still in awe. "But I was a bit nervous when he came near me to answer my query."

"He was so down-to-earth and approachable," added Druv.

"And his advice was so valuable," said Inaya.

"I feel like I have a better understanding of what it takes to succeed in the corporate world," said Sameer.

The students learned much today from Victor and were grateful for the opportunity to meet and talk with him. They knew that this was a conversation they would never forget and would always remember the valuable lessons they learned from the CEO himself.

Aarvi and Sameer headed toward the library while Druv and Inaya decided to return to their hostel.

The quiet and peaceful atmosphere greeted them as they entered the library. They found a table in a quiet corner and started going through their notes and papers.

Aarvi and Sameer discussed their presentations and offered each other feedback and suggestions. They found they had much in common, including their passion for sustainability and the environment.

"You know, I think our presentations complement each other well," said Aarvi. "We should present together."
"That's a great idea," said Sameer. "We could show how marketing and renewable energy are connected and how companies can benefit from both."

Aarvi and Sameer spent the next few hours working on their presentation, bouncing ideas off each other and fine-tuning their arguments. They were so focused that they overlooked the time flying by.

When they finally looked at the clock, they were surprised to see how late it was. "Wow, it's already past 9 pm," said Aarvi. "We should head back to the hostel."

"Yeah, we don't want to be too tired for our presentations tomorrow," said Sameer.

As they returned to the hostel, Aarvi and Sameer were full of energy and excitement. They were confident in their presentations and looked forward to presenting their ideas to the class. They said goodnight to each other and went to their respective rooms, ready to get some rest and prepare for the big day ahead.

At the other end, Druv and Inaya returned to their hostel after a long day. As they walked, they talked about their plans for the future.

"I enjoyed the CEO's lecture today," said Druv. "I want to start my career in finance someday and positively impact the world."

"That's great," said Inaya. "What kind of company do you like to join?"

"I'm still figuring that out," Druv replied. "But I'm interested in clean energy and sustainable products. I want to make a difference and leave a positive legacy."

Inaya nodded in agreement. "I want to do something similar in the HR department," she said. "I'm interested in fashion and sustainability. Someday I want to create a line of eco-friendly clothing that's stylish and affordable."

Druv smiled. "That's a fantastic idea. I think there's a real need for that in the market. You could make a real difference."

As they arrived at their hostel, they said goodnight to each other and went to their respective rooms. Druv and Inaya were tired from the long day but were inspired and motivated to pursue their dreams. They drifted off to sleep, dreaming of a better, more sustainable future.

Building a professional network

The sun shone brightly as Aarvi, Druv, Inaya, and Sameer made their way to the lecture hall of the prestigious B-School. They were all eager to learn more about the corporate world and were excited to hear the CEO, Victor Edmund, speak for the Third Day.

The walls were adorned with pictures of successful alums, including Victor Edmund. The stage was set with a podium and microphone. Aarvi, Druv, Inaya, and Sameer took their seats in the front row, ready to soak up every word Victor had to say.

The lecture started, and Victor stepped up to the podium. He was a tall man with a commanding presence, and the students were instantly captivated by his charisma and confidence.

Victor then started to talk about the importance of building a professional network.

He said, "Building a professional network is essential in helping you achieve your career goals. Investing in relationships with like-minded peers and mentors in your industry can provide you with knowledge, support, and guidance to help you succeed."

"Connecting to key individuals, firms, and organizations gives you access to up-to-date industry-specific news, recommendations, and advice that may not have been available anywhere else."

He paused and started, "Additionally, expanding your professional network can make job opportunities easier as you'll be the first in line when new positions arise. Finding ways to connect with professionals in your field or meeting experts through industry conferences are great starting points. Connecting with people within your field may seem intimidating but remember they started at the same place you are now! Take the opportunity today to help build a strong foundation for yourself professionally."

He then shared tips and strategies for expanding one's network, including attending events, reaching out to contacts, and using social media. Aarvi, Druv, Inaya, and Sameer paid close attention, took notes, and nodded in agreement.

As the lecture ended, Victor had a surprise in store.

Once the lecture hall had emptied, Victor asked Sameer, Inaya, Aarvi, and Druv to stay back. Students were eagerly looking forward to it. He turned to the students and said, "Aarvi, Druv, Inaya, and Sameer, I have taken notice of your eagerness to learn and drive to succeed. That is why I would like to offer you the opportunity to become my mentee. I want to help you reach your full potential and achieve your career aspirations."

The students were thrilled and couldn't wait to start working with Victor. Immediately they said yes, and soon they were on their way to start their mentorship with Victor.

"Come, let's sit towards the center of the stage and discuss." Victor invited all four of them. Aarvi was very eager, as usual. She asked, "Mr. Edmund, can you provide us with some great tips for building a professional network?"

"Of Course." Said Victor. "Let's look upon 3 major tips."

Victor adjusted his tie and coat and quickly checked the mobile.

Victor, "As the first tip, how about we talk about how to get the most out of attending events?"
Aarvi, "Sounds good to me, Mr. Edmund."

Victor, "Great! So the first thing I want you all to remember is to be prepared. Do your research on the event and the attendees beforehand. Know what you want to achieve and be ready to introduce yourself and share your goals and experiences."

Druv, "That makes sense. You don't want to show up to an event and be caught off guard."

Victor, " Exactly, Druv. The next thing I want to emphasize is dressing the part. Make a good first impression by dressing appropriately for the event. Your attire should reflect professionalism and show that you take the event seriously."

Victor, "The third tip is to be an active listener. Engage with others by asking questions and truly listening to their responses. Show an interest in their experiences and goals, and be open to learning from them. And don't forget to follow up after the event. Take the time to follow up with any new contacts you made. This could be as simple as sending an email to thank them for their time and reiterating your interest in connecting."

Aarvi, "That's a great reminder. And finally, don't be afraid to strike up conversations with strangers. You never know who you might meet and what opportunities arise from these connections."

Victor, "Exactly, Aarvi. These are the five ways to make the most of attending events. So, remember to be prepared, dress the part, be an active listener, follow up, and make connections."

"Ok, Let's take up an example," said Victor. "Aarvi, Let's start with you. Let's hear as you want to make an Impression in marketing. Would you like to learn some tips on how to make the most of attending events?"

Aarvi, "Yes, I would love that! I've been to a few events before but haven't had much success making meaningful connections."

Victor, "Well, don't worry. Let's review some tips to help you make the most of attending events. First, start by researching events relevant to your industry, such as marketing conferences, trade shows, or networking events. Check the agendas and speaker lists to determine which events would be the best fit for you."

Aarvi, "That's a great tip. I never thought to check the speaker lists."

Victor, "Exactly! And once you've selected a few events to attend, register for them in advance. This will allow you to connect with others before the event and build relationships."

Aarvi, "That makes sense. I'll start doing that."

Victor, "Good. Finally, before the event, create a 30-second elevator pitch introducing you, your profession, and what you hope to gain from it. This will help you make a great first impression and feel more confident when networking."

Victor continued, "When you arrive at the event, arrive early. This will give you time to settle in, grab a drink, and mingle with others before the official program begins. This is a great opportunity to start building relationships and making connections."

Victor, "Finally, once the event is underway, actively engage with others. This means introducing yourself, asking questions, and participating in networking activities or sessions."
Aarvi, "Ok, I'll be more proactive in engaging with others."

Victor, "Great! And after the event, follow up with the people you met by sending a quick email or LinkedIn message. Thank them for their time and let them know you enjoyed meeting them."

Aarvi, "Thank you. These tips are beneficial, and I can't wait to put them into practice."

"Now Tip - 2, which is reaching out to contact". Victor started with the next tip.

Victor, "So, the first step is to list all the people you know who could potentially introduce you to others in your industry. This could include former coworkers, classmates, friends, or even family members."

Inaya, "That's a great point. I never thought of contacting my family members for professional connections."

Victor, "Exactly, Inaya. You never know who might know someone in your industry, so it's important to cast a wide net. Once you have your list, the next step is to reach out to each person and let them know you want to expand your professional network. Ask if they know anyone in your industry to who they could introduce you. And it's important to remember that people are often happy to help others, so don't be afraid to reach out and ask. After you receive introductions, the next step is to follow up with the new contacts you made. Thank them for their time and let them know you're interested in connecting."

Sameer, "Yes, following up is crucial. I often forget to follow up after meeting new people, and that's a missed opportunity to strengthen a connection."

Victor, "Exactly, Sameer. And finally, once you've made new connections, make sure to keep in touch with them. This could be through regular email exchanges, attending industry events, or even reaching out every few months to check-in. And most importantly, always be gracious and appreciative of your contacts' time and effort in helping you expand your network. Offer to help them however you can, and return the favor by introducing them to others in your network."

Victor concluded, "By following these steps, you'll be well on your way to making valuable connections and expanding your professional network through reaching out to your contacts. Just remember to be confident, be yourself, and always be gracious and appreciative of the help others offer you."

Victor moved his gaze to Sameer. "Ok, Sameer, as a fresh graduate wanting to break into the IT field, one of the best things you can do is go out to your contacts."
Sameer, "Yes, that makes sense. How do I start?"

Victor, "Great question, Sameer. The first step is to identify your contacts. Make a list of everyone you know who works in the tech industry or who may know someone who does. This could include family members, friends, former coworkers, or professors. After you have your list, make a plan for how you're going to reach out to each contact. Decide whether you want to reach out through email, phone, or in-person coffee or lunch meetings, and schedule when you'll reach out to each person."

Victor continued, "It's important to be organized and intentional when contacting your contacts. When you reach out, please introduce yourself and tell them you're interested in breaking into the tech industry. Ask if they have any advice or know of any job openings, and thank them for their time. After you've made the initial contact, it's important to keep in touch with your contacts. This could mean sending them periodic updates on your job search or contacting them for informational interviews. And don't forget to help others as you build your professional network. This could mean making introductions, offering advice, or even helping others find job opportunities."

Sameer, "That's a lot of great advice, Victor. Thank you."
Victor, "You're welcome, Sameer. And don't forget, networking is all about building relationships and helping each other. So always be gracious and appreciative of your contacts' time and effort."

Aarvi was curious about the power of Social Media in networking, to which Victor replied enthuslastically, "That's my last but most essential tip!"

Victor elaborated, "Let's discuss using social media to build your professional network. As you know, social media is a tremendous tool for connecting with others in your business, showcasing your skills, and developing your professional brand. Here are some specific ways to make the most of it:

1. Be Active: To build a strong network, you must be active on social media. This means posting regularly, commenting on others' posts, and engaging with

your network. You want to be present and involved in the conversations in your industry.

2. Brand Yourself: Make sure your social media profiles accurately reflect your professional brand. This means using a professional headshot, crafting a clear and concise bio, and sharing relevant content for your industry. This is your digital footprint, and presenting yourself professionally is essential.

3. Connect with Others: Use social media to connect with others in your industry. Follow people you admire, participate in LinkedIn groups, and join Twitter chats. This is a great way to expand your network and connect with people interested in the same topics as you.

4. Share Your Expertise: Social media is an excellent platform for sharing your expertise and thought leadership. Share articles, blog posts, and other content that showcases your knowledge and experience. This will help you establish yourself as an expert in your field and build your brand.

5. Network Digitally: Social media provides an opportunity to network digitally. You can attend virtual events, connect with others in online groups, and participate in webinars. With so many opportunities to connect online, there's no reason not to use social media to build your professional network.

So, these are specific ways to make the most of social media for building your professional network. Remember, it takes time and effort, but if you're consistent and intentional, you'll be amazed at the results. Any questions so far, Aarvi, Sameer, Inaya, and Druv? "

Inaya was curious. She wanted to understand the concept through an example.

"Well, Good!!!" said the CEO. " Here is one for you."

"So, Inaya, the first step is to choose the right platforms. As a graphic designer, suppose you'll want to focus on platforms most relevant to your industry and target audience, such as Instagram, Behance, and LinkedIn."

"Next, optimize your social media profiles to accurately reflect your skills, experience, and portfolio. Use high-quality photos and a professional tone to present yourself in the best light possible. This will help you attract potential clients and stand out from the competition."

"Then, it's important to connect with others in your network. Follow other graphic designers, clients, and industry influencers, and engage with their posts to build relationships. Sharing your work regularly on social media is also a great way to showcase your skills and attract new clients."

He added, "Make sure to respond to comments and messages from your followers and engage with them meaningfully. This could mean answering questions, giving feedback, or conversing. By interacting with your followers, you'll build trust and connections that could lead to new business opportunities."

"Finally, attend online events and webinars related to your industry and participate in online discussions and chats. This will allow you to connect with others and learn about your field's latest trends and developments. By being active and engaged on social media, you'll be able to expand your client base and grow your business.
Inaya, do you have any questions or concerns about using social media to expand your client base?"

Inaya nodded to say no. " I think it is pretty clear now."

Victor sat in his chair, looking at the clock on the wall. The students were preparing to return to their evening classes, but he had something important to tell them. He called Aarvi, Inaya, Druv, and Sameer closer.
"Ok, guys, I just wanted to let you know that I have to return to London tonight," said Victor. "I'll be back next week, but I want you to keep working hard on all the points I told you."

Aarvi, Inaya, Druv, and Sameer looked at each other, surprised. They had grown so used to Victor being around that they hadn't even thought about him leaving so suddenly.

"That's so sudden, sir," said Inaya.
Druv said, "But sir, what if we have any questions or need help?"

"Just remember all the lessons I've taught you," said Victor. "And if you need help, you can always reach out to me via email. I'll be checking my inbox regularly."

"Ok, sir, we'll keep working hard," said Aarvi.

"Good," said Victor, standing up from his desk. "Now, let's get back to work. I have a plane to catch."

The students said goodbye to Victor, who grabbed his briefcase and headed out the door. As they watched him go, they couldn't help but feel slightly sad. But they also felt motivated to continue the work he had started with them. They knew that they could achieve anything they set their minds to with Victor's guidance.

Understanding the job market and job search strategies

Aarvi, Inaya, Druv, and Sameer were over the moon with excitement. It had been a whole week since they had last seen their favorite charismatic leader, Victor Edmund, in the lecture hall. Despite the short break from his lecture series, the four students felt like an entire year had passed.

They had been working hard on the tips and advice that Victor had given them during his last lecture, and they couldn't wait to hear what he had in store for them today.
As they walked into the lecture hall, they could feel the buzz of excitement in the air. Students chattered and laughed, eager to see Victor back at the podium.

Victor arrived in style. But this time, it was different. He had a calm, confident air about him. He knew something that the rest of them did not.
Striding up to the podium with his briefcase, he proclaimed in a solid yet triumphant voice, "Good Morning! I am overjoyed to be back here as promised."

He then stopped and scanned the room, searching for his favorite students.

Before going further, he called Aarvi, Inaya, Druv, and Sameer to the front of the podium. The four students' hearts skipped a beat as they approached the podium. He leaned towards them and smiled.

"I have an appointment with some business teams tomorrow," Victor said, "so I won't be able to personally sit with you today. But I promise to be as elaborative as possible in today's lecture so that all of you can understand."

Aarvi, Inaya, Druv, and Sameer were disappointed. Still, they were grateful for Victor's extra effort in today's lecture.
Victor began speaking, and the students were captivated by his charisma and energy. His words were filled with wisdom and experience, and the students could feel inspired by his every word.

He fine-tuned the microphone and began his lengthy address.

As you begin your job search, you must understand the employment market and the numerous tactics available to discover your next career opportunity. Whether you are a recent graduate or a seasoned professional, finding the right job can be challenging and competitive. But with the right tools and strategies, you can increase your chances of success and land your dream job.

Understanding the Job Market

The job market is a dynamic and ever-changing landscape that requires constant attention and adaptation. With new industries and job opportunities popping up daily, staying informed and knowledgeable about the job market and its trends is essential. This will help you identify the best career opportunities and position yourself for success.

It's essential to research the latest job market trends. You can do this by reading industry publications, following relevant news sources, and keeping current with job market statistics. For example, you may be interested in learning which job titles, such as data analyst or software engineer, are in great demand and which industries, such as technology or healthcare, are experiencing considerable development. Knowing current trends will assist you in determining where your talents and interests connect with the employment market, allowing you to focus your career search.

In addition to general job market trends, it's also important to research specific industries and companies that interest you. For example, suppose you have a passion for environmental sustainability. In that case, you may want to research companies at the forefront of this movement, such as Patagonia or Tesla. By exploring these companies, you can better understand their values, culture, and hiring processes. You can also learn about career roles and responsibilities in the business, such as those of an environmental scientist or a renewable energy specialist, and the qualifications and experience needed for those positions.

Researching the job market and industries is crucial in your job search journey. It will help you identify the best opportunities and position yourself for success. By staying informed and knowledgeable, you can make informed decisions about your career and take advantage of the exciting job opportunities available.

Preparing a Strong Resume and Cover Letter

Your resume and cover letter are the first impression you make on potential employers, so getting them right is essential. These documents are your opportunity to showcase your skills, experience, and achievements and demonstrate why you're the right candidate for the job. Here's how to prepare a strong resume and cover letter that will grab the attention of hiring managers and help you stand out from the competition.

Starting with your resume, creating a clear and concise document showcasing your strengths and accomplishments is essential. Start by including relevant work experience, education, and skills. Remember to highlight your achievements, such as leading a successful project, winning a company award, or completing a relevant certification. Use keywords and phrases relevant to the job you're applying for. This will help your resume get noticed by both humans and applicant tracking systems (ATS).

Regarding your cover letter, it's important to personalize and tailor it to the company and position you're applying for. Start by explaining why you're interested in the company, the role, and how your skills and experience align with their requirements. Provide specific examples of your achievements, such as increasing sales by 20% or streamlining a process to improve efficiency. Highlight the unique value you can bring to the company, such as your passion for innovation or ability to think outside the box.

Your resume and cover letter allow you to make a strong impression on potential employers and demonstrate why you're the right candidate for the job. By focusing on creating a clear, concise, and compelling document, you can increase your chances of getting noticed and landing your dream job.

Finding Job Opportunities

Finding job opportunities can be a challenge, but with the right strategy and approach, it can be a rewarding experience. Here are some examples of how you can effectively search for job opportunities:

Utilizing Online Job Boards: Sarah was a recent college graduate with a degree in Marketing. She was intensely interested in the tech industry and wanted to work for a startup. Sarah began her job search using online job boards such as Indeed and LinkedIn. She created job alerts for marketing positions in the IT business. She narrowed down the results based on geography and wage expectations... Sarah could find several job openings that fit her criteria and applied to them. One of her applications was successful, and she landed a job as a Marketing Associate at a fast-growing tech startup.

Exploring Company Websites: Mark was an experienced software engineer who wanted to work for a company that values innovation and creativity. He did his research and identified several companies that fit his criteria. He then visited the company websites and found that many had career pages listing job openings and company culture. Mark was able to find a job opening that matched his skills and experience and applied to it. He got an interview and was eventually offered the job. He was thrilled to start working for a company he admired and respected.

Leveraging Professional Networks: Rachel was an HR professional who wanted to change and find a new job opportunity. She contacted her network of friends and colleagues in the HR industry and asked for their advice and recommendations. One of her friends referred her to a recruiter specializing in HR positions. The recruiter helped Rachel update her resume and connect with companies that were hiring HR professionals. Rachel could find a job that she was passionate about and offered a better work-life balance.

Attending Job Fairs: Jake recently graduated with a degree in Business Administration. He wanted to work for a large corporation in the financial industry. Jake attended a job fair for the financial industry and met with several recruiters from different companies. He was able to learn about the job requirements and company culture, and he also had the opportunity to network with other professionals in his field. Jake landed a job as a Financial Analyst at a well-known corporation thanks to his participation in the job fair.

Victor added, "These are just a few examples of how you can effectively search for job opportunities and find a job that aligns with your skills, experience, and career goals. You may boost your chances of success and finding a job you enjoy by researching the job market, writing a solid CV and cover letter, and looking for work openings.."

Pausing to take a sip of water, he concluded, "Since I have other obligations for the day, why don't we wrap up here and pick this conversation back up tomorrow?"

The four friends were amazed at how thorough Victor was. Every minute detail was accounted for in his presentation. He never skipped over essential points and didn't gloss over anything that some students didn't understand. His charisma filled the room with infectious energy. Everyone in the audience felt captivated by him and motivated to progress further.

By the end of his presentation, everyone, including Aarvi, Inaya, Druv, and Sameer, felt energized and ready to take on whatever challenges may come their way. They couldn't wait for Victor to return so they could benefit further from his wisdom.

Despite their displeasure at not being able to sit with Victor one-on-one for the day, four believed that today's lecture was more beneficial than any one-on-one session.
As the lecture ended, Aarvi and Sameer went to the nearby shop to purchase supplies for their next assignment. They walked through the bustling streets, their heads filled with the ideas and inspiration Victor shared in his lecture.

On the other hand, Inaya and Druv decided to stay behind in the lecture hall. They wanted to talk to the other students and see how they felt about Victor's lecture. As they mingled and chatted, they were amazed by Victor's impact on their peers. Everyone talked about the wisdom and inspiration he had shared and how he had left a lasting impression on them all.

"I never knew a lecture could be so engaging," one student said, "Victor knows how to connect with the audience."

"He's a true magician," another student added, "the way he can take complex ideas and make them, so simple to understand is truly amazing."

Inaya and Druv nodded in agreement, proud to have such a talented and inspiring CEO as their mentor. When they returned from the shop, they couldn't wait to share their thoughts and experiences with Aarvi and Sameer.

As they continued to mingle and chat with the other students, Inaya and Druv felt a sense of pride and camaraderie. They were part of a unique community, brought together by their shared love and respect for Victor. When Aarvi and Sameer returned from the shop, they could see the excitement in Inaya and Druv's eyes. They sat down and discussed the lecture, sharing their thoughts and experiences. The four friends were in awe of their mentor, and they couldn't wait to see what other lessons he had in store for them.

Resume and Cover Letter Writing

The sun had barely risen, and Aarvi, Inaya, Druv, and Sameer were in their classroom, excitedly expecting the mystery letter Victor's office had brought them that morning.

The four sat around the table, eyes wide with anticipation and curiosity. They all knew what this letter could mean for them and why Victor wanted them to be present when it opened.

"What do you think it could be?" Aarvi asked, breaking the silence.

"Maybe it's an invitation to a secret adventure!" Inaya said, her eyes shining with excitement.

"Or a treasure hunt," Druv added.

Sameer, who was always practical, said, "I doubt it. It looks more like a formal letter."

They all fell silent again as they stared at the letter, trying to figure out what it could be. Suddenly, Aarvi spoke up.
"I have an idea. Let's read it out loud."

The others nodded in agreement, and Aarvi began to read the letter.

"Dear Aarvi, Inaya, Druv, and Sameer," Aarvi began, "I am writing to inform you of an exciting opportunity. As you may know, yesterday I closed the lecture series quickly to meet a business team, and today I am free and wanted all of you to join me after class. The location is a secret that only the Director of your institution knows. I have arranged a vehicle to take you there along with him. Be ready by 3 P.M."

The friends looked at each other in shock and excitement. This was the adventure they had been waiting for!

"We're going, right?" Inaya asked, looking around at the others.

"Of course!" Druv replied. "This is exactly what we've been looking for."

"I agree," Sameer said. "We can't pass up an opportunity like this."
Aarvi nodded. "I'm in too. Let's do this!"

With anticipation and excitement, the friends made their way to Victor's car at 3 P.M sharp for the secret location outside Bengaluru.

Aarvi, Inaya, Druv, and Sameer were friends, always looking for adventure and excitement. Through the forest and mountain, they reached a secluded mountain retreat owned by Victor Edmund himself, and they couldn't resist the opportunity to explore it. They had all heard rumors of the beauty and serenity of the place, but they had no idea what they were in for.

As they made their way up the mountain, they felt a sense of anticipation and excitement. The journey was swift, but the scenery was breathtaking. They could see the rolling hills and valleys stretching before them, dotted with trees and wildlife. Finally, they arrived at the retreat, greeted by Victor's Assistant. She was a friendly, warm young lady who showed them inside Victor's temporary office.

Once inside, Victor greeted them warmly and gestured for them to sit at the table. "Please, sit," he said. "We have much to discuss."

Aarvi, Inaya, Druv, and Sameer sat down and looked around the room, taking in the stunning view from the window. Victor was a striking figure with sharp features and an impeccable sense of style. He was well known for his business acumen, but he also had a passion for adventure and a love of the great outdoors.

"So," Victor began, "I've heard you four are interested in exploring this place. I must say, I am impressed. Most people shy away from the unknown, but you seem to embrace it."
"Yes," Inaya spoke up. "We love adventure and heard that this place was special. We couldn't resist the opportunity to see it for ourselves."

Victor nodded, a twinkle in his eye. "Well, I must say, you won't be disappointed. This place is truly unique. It combines natural beauty and modern amenities, a true mountain oasis."

"We're eager to see it," Druv added.

"And I'm eager to show it to you," Victor replied. "But first, we must discuss some important matters."

The group leaned forward, intrigued by what Victor had to say. They listened as he laid out his plan for the day on resume development and covering letter writing.
"So, what do you say?" Victor asked, looking at each of them in turn.

Aarvi, Inaya, Druv, and Sameer looked at each other and then back at Victor, a smile spreading across their faces. "We're in and very much eager to hear your wisdom," they said in unison.

Inaya was a bit nervous and looked at Victor across from her. She had been looking forward to it, as she was eager to learn from the best in the field.

"Mr. Victor, I've been working on my resume for weeks now, but I just can't seem to get it right," Inaya said, looking at Victor with frustration and hope.

Victor nodded, understanding the importance of a well-crafted resume. "I understand your concerns, Inaya. What specifically are you struggling with?" he asked, leaning forward in his chair.

"Well, I don't know what to include or leave out. I have a lot of work experience, but I'm not sure if it's all relevant to the job I'm applying for," Inaya replied, shaking slightly.

Victor nodded, his expression serious. "You're not alone in this, Inaya. Many people struggle with the same thing. The key is to focus on your strengths and achievements rather than just listing your responsibilities. Highlight your accomplishments in each role and how they can benefit your future employer."

Victor continued, "As the job market becomes increasingly competitive, the pressure to create an effective resume and cover letter has never been greater. Whether starting your career or looking for a change, your resume and cover letter are your chance to make a strong first impression and stand out from the competition. We'll explore key elements in writing an effective resume and cover letter, including what to include, what to avoid, and how to make the most of your experience."

"When writing your resume, it's important to remember that it should be concise, clear, and focused. Your objective is to create a document showcasing your skills, experience, and achievements while highlighting your potential as a candidate. You should include your work history, education, and relevant certifications or training to achieve this. You should also highlight your most significant accomplishments and skills, and include keywords relevant to the position you're applying for."

"When writing an effective resume, it's important to understand that the document you create should be a concise, clear, and focused representation of your skills, experience, and achievements. Creating a document showcasing your potential as a candidate increases your chances of landing an interview and, ultimately, the job."

Here are some essential dos and don'ts to keep in mind when writing your resume:

Do's:

1. Tailor your resume to the specific job and company. Use keywords from the job description, and highlight skills and experiences relevant to the position you're applying for.

2. Use clear, concise language. Your resume should be easy to read and understand, with no spelling or grammar errors.

3. Include your work history, education, and any relevant certifications or training. Be sure to include dates, job titles, and the names of the companies you worked for.

4. Highlight your most significant accomplishments and skills. Use specific examples to illustrate your points, and quantify your achievements whenever possible.

5. Make use of an appropriate format. Consider using a professional resume template or seeking advice from a career counselor to ensure your resume is formatted professionally.

Don'ts:

1. Include irrelevant information. Your resume should focus on your job qualifications, and any information that doesn't contribute to that goal should be left out.

2. Use generic language. Avoid using phrases like "responsible for" or "duties included." Instead,

highlight your achievements and explain your impact on your previous employers.

3. Neglect proofreading and editing. Ensure your resume is free of spelling and grammar errors and is formatted professionally.

4. Use a self-serving tone. Your resume should be focused on what you can offer the company, not what the company can offer you.

5. Lie or exaggerate your achievements. Be honest about your skills and experience, and highlight your strengths rather than making false claims.

Finally, Victor said, "By following these dos and don'ts, you can create a concise, clear, and focused resume that showcases your skills, experience, and achievements in the best possible light. With the right approach, you can create a document to help you stand out from the competition and increase your chances of landing an interview."

Aarvi nodded, taking notes as Victor continued. "And when it comes to the layout and design of your resume, make sure it's visually appealing and easy to read. Use bullet points and clear, concise language. You want to ensure your potential employer can quickly see your skills and experience."

Victor then pulled out a few examples of well-written resumes and went through each with Inaya, pointing out the strengths and weaknesses of each. Inaya was amazed at how much she had learned from this meeting with Victor.

Victor was elaborate. He further reached out to his desk to pull some templates.

"For example, Aarvi, your interest in marketing should reflect in your resume. You can develop a similar resume like this."

[Your Name]
[Address]
[Phone Number]
[Email Address]

Objective: A highly motivated and results-driven marketing professional with an assertive consumer behavior and market research background seeking a challenging and dynamic marketing role where I can utilize my skills and knowledge to drive business growth.

Education: MBA in Marketing, [University Name], [Graduation Date] Bachelor of Science in Business Administration, [University Name], [Graduation Date]

Skills:

- *Market research and analysis*

- *Consumer behavior analysis*

- *Brand management*

- *Marketing strategy development*

- *Data analysis and interpretation*

- *Project management*

- *Strong communication and interpersonal skills*

- *Proficient in Microsoft Office, Google Analytics, and Marketo*

Work Experience: Marketing Intern, [Company Name], [City, State], [Dates of Employment]

- Conducted market research and consumer behavior analysis to support the development of marketing strategies

- Assisted in the execution of digital marketing campaigns, including email, social media, and paid advertising

- Conducted data analysis and interpreted results to measure the effectiveness of marketing efforts

- Collaborated with cross-functional teams, including sales, product development, and creative, to drive project success

- Contributed to the development of presentations and reports to communicate insights and recommendations to stakeholders

Volunteer Experience: Marketing Volunteer, [Non-Profit Organization Name], [City, State], [Dates of Status]
- Provided support to the marketing team in the development and execution of marketing campaigns

- Conducted market research to gather insights into target audiences and consumer behavior

- Contributed to the development of presentations and reports to communicate insights and recommendations to stakeholders

Certifications:
- Google Analytics

- Marketo Certified Expert

References: Available upon request.

"And Sameer, I suggest you get some work experience before you start your venture. This is the era of Startups, but most of the startup's success lies with its founders. Hence, let's say you want to gain experience in a tech company. Your resume should look something similar to this." He took out another template.

[Your Name]
[Address]
[Phone Number]
[Email Address]

Objective: A highly motivated and technically skilled MBA graduate seeking a challenging role in a dynamic tech company where I can utilize my technical and business knowledge to drive growth and innovation.
Education: MBA in Business Technology, [University Name], [Graduation Date] Bachelor of Science in Computer Science, [University Name], [Graduation Date]
Skills:

- *Technical project management*

- *Business strategy development*

- *Business process improvement*

- *Data analysis and interpretation*

- *Proficient in SQL, Python, and Tableau*

- *Strong communication and interpersonal skills*

- *Experience with Agile methodology*

- *Knowledge of cloud computing and DevOps*

Work Experience: Tech Intern, [Company Name], [City, State], [Dates of Employment]

- *Assisted in the planning and execution of technical projects for clients*

- *Conducted data analysis to measure the effectiveness of technical solutions and provide insights for improvement*

- *Worked with cross-functional teams, including development, product, and business, to drive project success*

- *Contributed to the development of presentations and reports to communicate insights and recommendations to stakeholders*

Volunteer Experience: Tech Volunteer, [Non-Profit Organization Name], [City, State], [Dates of Status]

- *Provided technical support and solutions to non-profit organizations*

- *Assisted in the planning and execution of technical projects*

- *Contributed to the development of presentations and reports to communicate insights and recommendations to stakeholders*

Certifications:

- *AWS Certified Solutions Architect*

- *Certified Scrum Master*

References: Available upon request.

Victor quickly added, "Please note that this is just an example. The content can vary based on the individual's experience and qualifications."

"Remember, Inaya," Victor said as they glanced further. "Your resume is your first impression, so take the time to make it strong."

As Victor was finishing his advice to Inaya on resume writing, Druv interrupted with his own question.

"Excuse me, Mr. Victor, but I have a question about cover letter writing," Druv said, his eyes lighting up with interest. "I've always struggled with writing cover letters, and I'm hoping you can help me."

Victor smiled, happy to help another aspiring job seeker. "Of course, Druv. What would you like to know?"

"Well, I've heard that cover letters are becoming less important these days," Druv said, looking at Victor for confirmation.

Victor shook his head. "Not at all. While it's true that some companies may not place as much emphasis on cover letters, it's still an important tool for making a strong first impression. It's a chance to show your personality and explain why you're the best fit for the job."

Druv nodded, taking in Victor's words. "Okay, so what should I include in my cover letter?"

"First, you want to address the hiring manager by name," Victor said. "You can usually find this information on the company's website or through a quick Google search. Next, explain why you're interested in the company and the specific role you're applying for. Remember to highlight your relevant skills and experience and explain how they align with the job requirements."

Victor added, "Your cover letter is also critical to your job application. It should be just as focused and targeted as your resume. Your cover letter aims to explain why you're the best candidate for the position and how your skills and experience match the job requirements. To achieve this, you should address the employer's specific needs, explain how your experience is relevant to the position, and highlight the value you can bring to the company."

"When writing your cover letter, avoiding common pitfalls like using generic language, repeating information from your resume, or making baseless claims is important. Instead, it would be best to focus on making a strong, personal connection with the employer and demonstrating your unique skills and qualities. To make the most of your cover letter, use specific examples to illustrate your points, and tailor your writing style to match the tone of the company and the job posting."

Victor then goes over the dos and don'ts. "It's vital to remember while writing your cover letter that it's not just a reiteration of your resume, but rather a customized and intriguing introduction that sets you apart from the competition."

"Here are some essential tips to keep in mind when writing your cover letter:

Do's:

1. Address the hiring manager by name. If the job posting lists a specific person, use their name. If not, take the time to research the company and find out who the hiring manager is.

2. Tailor your cover letter to the specific job and company. Mention specific details from the job posting and explain how your skills and experience match what the company seeks.

3. Use specific examples to illustrate your points. Provide concrete examples of your achievements, skills, and experience that are relevant to the job.

4. Show your enthusiasm for the company and the position. Please explain why you're interested in the company and excited about the opportunity to join their team.

5. Keep it concise and focused. Your cover letter should be no more than one page and focus on making a solid case for why you're the best candidate for the job.

Don'ts:

1. Repeat the information from your resume. Your cover letter should complement your resume, not repeat it.

2. Use generic language. Avoid phrases like "I am writing to express my interest in the position" or "I am a

hard worker and a team player." These statements are overused and lack originality.

3. Make baseless claims. Don't make exaggerated or false statements about your skills and experience. Instead, highlight your accomplishments and explain how they make you a strong candidate.

4. Use a formal, stuffy tone. Your cover letter should reflect your personality and writing style but also match the tone of the company and the job posting.

5. Neglect proofreading and editing. Make sure your cover letter is free of spelling and grammar errors and is formatted professionally."

"By following these dos and don'ts, you can create an engaging, personalized, and effective cover letter. Remember, your cover letter is your chance to make a strong first impression and demonstrate your enthusiasm and qualifications for the job. With the right approach, you can write a cover letter to help you stand out from the competition and increase your chances of landing an interview." Victor closed his tips.

Victor then pulled out a few examples of cover letters and went through each one with Druv, pointing out the strengths and weaknesses of each. Druv was impressed with the detail and care that went into each cover letter. He felt much more confident about his cover letter writing skills.

Victor was ready with a template to share. He said, "For example, your covering letter may look similar," and passed them to students.

Dear [Hiring Manager's Name],

I am writing to express my interest in the [Job Title] position at [Company Name]. As a recent graduate with a [Degree and Field of Study] from [University Name], I am eager to bring my skills and passion to a challenging and dynamic work environment.

My coursework, relevant internships, and volunteer experiences have equipped me with a strong foundation in [Key Skills or Competencies]. In particular, my experience as a [Relevant Internship or Volunteer Role] at [Company Name or Organization] allowed me to apply these skills in a real-world setting. I was responsible for [Key Achievements or Contributions] and learned the importance of [Key Lessons or Skills].

I am confident that my skills and experiences make me a strong fit for the [Job Title] role at [Company Name]. I am particularly drawn to your company's commitment to [Company Value or Mission]. I am excited to contribute to your team's efforts.

In addition to my technical skills, I am a quick learner, a strong communicator, and a dedicated team player. I am committed to delivering high-quality work and going above and beyond to meet your company's needs.

Thank you for considering my application. I am eager to further discuss my qualifications and how I can contribute to [Company Name]. I look forward to hearing back from you soon.

Sincerely, [Your Name]

Victor concluded, "Writing an effective resume and cover letter requires a strategic approach and attention to detail. You can make a positive first impression and boost your chances of winning your dream job by focusing on the main aspects that make up a successful document and avoiding frequent blunders. Remember, your resume and cover letter are your chance to make a statement about who you are and what you have to offer, so take the time to create a document that reflects your skills, experience, and potential. With the right approach, you can write a resume and cover letter to help you stand out from the competition and achieve your professional goals."

The four friends looked at each other, each eager to speak but unsure who should start. Finally, Aarvi took a deep breath and said, "That was a piece of great advice. We never had any help. Thank You."

Victor nodded, a twinkle in his eye. "I understand," he said. "And I have a special treat for you all. How about I give you a tour of my mountain retreat? It's a beautiful, secluded place where I go to get away from the hustle and bustle of the city. It will be a great setting for us to talk and learn."

Aarvi, Inaya, Druv, and Sameer looked excitedly at each other. They had heard about Victor's retreat but never expected to have the chance to visit it themselves.

"That sounds amazing," Druv said, his voice filled with enthusiasm. "We'd love to take you up on that offer, Mr. Victor."

Victor smiled and stood up from his chair. "Perfect," he said. "Let's go. The scenery is breathtaking, and I think you'll find the tour both educational and inspirational."

With that, the group set off on their journey to the retreat, eager to learn all they could from Victor and soak up the beauty of the surrounding mountains. They knew this was an opportunity of a lifetime and were determined to make the most of it.

As the group of four students, Aarvi, Inaya, Druv, and Sameer, followed Victor and his assistant on the tour of the mountain retreat, they were in awe of the breathtaking scenery surrounding them. The sun was about to set, glowing warmly on the lush green forests and towering peaks.

"This place is simply amazing," Aarvi exclaimed, taking in the views. "I've never seen anything like it."

"I'm glad you're enjoying it," Victor smiled. "The retreat was designed to provide a serene environment for reflection and inspiration. We believe that the surroundings can powerfully impact the mind and soul."

As they continued their tour, the group marveled at the unique architecture and design of the retreat's buildings. Victor took them inside one of the structures, a large meditation hall with a high ceiling and floor-to-ceiling windows. The peaceful ambiance struck the group, and Inaya couldn't help but remark, "This place truly feels like a sanctuary."

Next, the group was shown the outdoor arena, where Victor explained that many workshops and events were held. The arena was surrounded by nature, and the group could hear the gentle sound of a nearby stream.

"This place is truly a hidden gem," Druv commented. "I can't believe how beautiful it is."

As the tour ended, the group thanked Victor and his assistant for the wonderful experience. They promised to cherish the tour's memories and the retreat's inspiring atmosphere.

As the sun set over the mountains, Aarvi, Inaya, Druv, and Sameer returned to Victor's office, eager to thank him for his time and insights.

"Thank you so much for showing us around the retreat, Mr. Victor," Inaya said warmly. "We appreciate all the advice you've given us on resume and cover letter writing. It will be so helpful as we look for jobs after graduation."

Victor beamed with pride, happy to have positively impacted the students. "You're all very talented young people," he said. "I'm sure you'll make a big splash in your respective fields."

Druv, Aarvi, and Sameer nodded in agreement, grateful for the encouragement.

"It was great meeting you, Mr. Victor," Aarvi said, holding her hand. "We'll take everything you've taught us to heart."

Victor took each of their hands in turn, giving them a firm handshake. "Take care, and best of luck to all of you. I will meet all of you tomorrow at the college cafeteria. If you need further details, don't hesitate to reach out."

With that, the four friends said their final goodbyes and set off down the mountain, the stars shining bright above them. They chatted excitedly about all the lessons they had learned and the bright future ahead of them.

As they arrived back at the college, Aarvi, Inaya, Druv, and Sameer knew that their journey to the mountain retreat had been a turning point in their careers. They were now more confident, knowledgeable, and ready to take on the world. And they knew that they had Victor to thank for it all.

Acing the Interview

It was a cold Monday morning at the prestigious business school, and the students eagerly anticipated Victor Edmund's lecture on job interviews. Aarvi, Inaya, Druv, and Sameer huddled in the corridor outside the lecture hall, discussing their expectations for the session.

"I hope he gives us some practical tips on how to ace job interviews," said Aarvi, adjusting her glasses nervously.
"Yeah, and it would be great if he could give us some insights on handling tricky interview questions," added Inaya, sipping her coffee.

Victor emerged from the lecture hall and spotted the group as they were talking. He had a surprise in store for them and beckoned them over.

"Hey, you four! Come over here. I have something special for you," he said, a twinkle in his eye.

Victor leaned in. "I want you to come to the cafeteria early this evening, dressed professionally. I'll be there to give you some last-minute coaching and practice interviews."

Sameer nodded eagerly. "What time should we be there?"

"Be there at 6 pm sharp," Victor instructed. "And make sure you're dressed to impress. This could be the opportunity of a lifetime."

Druv grinned. "We won't let you down, Victor."

As they walked away, Aarvi couldn't believe their luck. She had always dreamed of working at a top marketing firm but never thought it was possible. Now, with Victor's help, it seemed within reach.

Little did they know that they were in for an unforgettable experience. The evening at the cafeteria would test their skills, nerves, and determination. But one thing was sure, they were ready for whatever came their way.

The four students, Aarvi, Inaya, Druv, and Sameer, eagerly made their way to the business school cafeteria, where they were scheduled to meet with their favorite CEO, Victor Edmund. As they approached the cafeteria, they couldn't help but notice a stunning lady dressed in a power suit deep in conversation with Victor.

"Who's that?" whispered Aarvi, nudging Inaya.

"I don't know," replied Inaya, "but she looks important."

As Victor noticed the group of students approaching, he smiled and excused himself from the lady. "Hey, guys! I'm glad you could make it," he said, giving each of them a firm handshake.

Before the students could say anything, Victor began introducing the lady. "This is Dayita Joseph," he said, gesturing towards her. "She is a friend of mine, and she's the Head of Human Resources at a leading automotive company based out of Mumbai. We are almost meeting after 10 years."

Dayita turned to face the group, and they couldn't help but be struck by her strong presence and air of competence. She looked at each of them and gave them a warm smile. "It's great to meet you all," she said. "Victor has told me so much about you."

The students were impressed by how quickly Dayita had made them feel at ease. It was clear that she knew how to connect with people and build rapport. Victor told Dayita how these four ambitious students prepared for job interviews, and Dayita's face lit up.

"Job interviews, huh?" she said with genuine enthusiasm. "Well, I'd be happy to help you guys out. I've got plenty of experience in that area, and I'd love to share some tips and tricks with you."

The students couldn't believe their luck. They had come to meet with their favorite CEO, and now they had the opportunity to be mentored by a seasoned professional like Dayita. They thanked her profusely, and Dayita gave them a reassuring smile.

"Don't worry, guys," she said. "I've got your back."

The students sat down eagerly, ready to soak up all the knowledge Dayita had to offer. "We are eager to learn. Where do we start?" asked Druv, leaning forward in his chair.

"Well, preparation is key," said Dayita, leaning back in her chair. "Preparing for an interview is crucial in setting yourself up for success. In addition to researching the company and the position, you can do several other things to prepare for your interview.

A critical aspect of preparation is practicing your responses to common interview questions. By doing this, you'll be able to articulate your experiences and skills more effectively during the actual interview. It's essential to tailor your responses to the job you're applying for and the company's culture and goals."

She continued, "Another helpful strategy is to review your resume and cover letter before the interview. This will help you recall specific accomplishments and experiences that you can use to answer interview questions. Be sure to highlight any skills or experiences that are particularly relevant to the job you're applying for."

She paused, looked at Victor, and added, "In addition, it's a good idea to research the interviewer, if possible. Check out their LinkedIn profile or other social media accounts to learn more about their background and experience. This can help you feel more comfortable during the interview and may provide valuable insights into what the interviewer is looking for in a candidate."

"Finally, arrive at the interview location early, so you have time to relax and collect your thoughts. Bring a copy of your resume and other relevant documents, such as a portfolio or work samples. This will demonstrate that you're well-prepared and organized."

The students nodded in agreement, taking notes as Dayita spoke.

"And what about what to wear?" asked Sameer, looking down at his shoe.

Dayita smiled at the four students and said, "Now that we've discussed how to prepare for an interview let's talk about what to wear. Dressing appropriately is crucial in making a positive first impression on your potential employer."

Druv asked, "What should men wear to an interview?"

"For men, a classic suit and tie in a neutral color, such as navy or black, is the most appropriate attire for a formal or corporate interview. Make sure your suit fits well and is comfortable to wear. Pair it with a dress shirt in a light color, and make sure your shoes are polished and match the color of your suit. Avoid flashy accessories or anything that distracts from your professional appearance," Dayita explained.

Inaya asked, "And what about women? What should we wear?"

"For women, a business suit or a conservative dress in a neutral color, such as black, navy, or gray, is the most appropriate attire for a formal or corporate interview. Avoid anything too tight or revealing, and wear closed-toe shoes with a low heel. Keep jewelry and accessories to a minimum, and avoid anything too flashy or distracting," Dayita advised. Aarvi then asked, "What if we're a little overweight? What kind of clothing should we wear?"

Dayita nodded and said, "If you're a little overweight, choosing clothes that flatter your body type is important. For men, a well-fitted suit that isn't too tight or loose is the best choice. Opt for darker colors, such as navy or black, and avoid anything too baggy or oversized. For women, choose clothing that fits well and flatters your figure. Look for clothes with a structured cut, such as jackets or blouses with defined waistlines, to create a more flattering silhouette. Avoid anything too tight or clingy, and opt for darker colors as they can be more slimming."

Sameer asked, "What kind of clothing should we avoid wearing to an interview?"

"Good question, Sameer. Avoid anything too casual, such as jeans, t-shirts, and sneakers. Even if the company culture is more relaxed, it's still important to dress professionally for the interview. Avoid anything too revealing or provocative, such as mini-skirts, crop tops, and low-cut blouses. Choose clothing that covers your body appropriately and doesn't show too much skin. Avoid anything too flashy or attention-grabbing, and don't wear anything with offensive language or symbols," Dayita explained.

"Thank you for these tips, Dayita. Dressing appropriately for an interview is an important factor we need to consider," Druv said, expressing his gratitude.

The other students nodded in agreement, thanking Dayita for her valuable advice.

"And what about answering common interview questions?" asked Aarvi.

Dayita, "One of the most common questions you'll be asked is, "Can you tell me a little about yourself?" This is an opportunity for the interviewer to get to know you better and for you to make a positive first impression."

Aarvi, "Ok, that makes sense. But what kind of information should I include in my answer?"

Dayita, "You want to focus on your professional background, skills, and experience. Keep it professional and relevant to the position you're applying for. While it's ok to share some personal details, such as hobbies or interests, the focus should be on your professional qualifications."

Inaya, "That sounds easy enough, but how long should my answer be?"

Dayita, "You should be concise and to the point. You don't need to go into great detail, as you'll have the opportunity to expand on your experience later in the interview. A good rule of thumb is to keep your answer under two minutes."

Druv, "That's helpful. But what if I don't have much experience in the field?"

Dayita, "Even if you don't have direct experience, you can still highlight transferable skills and accomplishments from other areas. This is a chance to showcase your strengths and show how they can benefit the company."

Sameer, "I understand that, but what else can I do to prepare for this question?"

Dayita, "It's always a good idea to practice your answer beforehand to feel confident and prepared when it comes up in the interview. You want to make sure your answer is tailored to the specific position you're applying for and that you can showcase how your background makes you a strong candidate for the job. The first question in a job interview is an opportunity to make a positive first impression and set the tone for the rest of the interview. By keeping your answer professional, concise, and tailored to the position you're applying for, you can make a strong impression on the interviewer and increase your chances of landing the job."

Dayita, "So, the next question you might face in your job interview is, "Why do you want to work for this company?" Have any of you heard this question before?"

Inaya, "Yes, I have. I always find it challenging to answer."

Druv, "Same here. I never know how to express my interest in the company without sounding too generic."

Dayita, "That's understandable. It can be tricky to strike the right balance. But, the key is to research the company and show enthusiasm for their work. For example, what do you like about the company, Aarvi?"

Aarvi, " I appreciate the company's focus on sustainability. I read that they have significantly reduced their carbon footprint, which aligns with my values."

Dayita, "That's a great point. And what about you, Druv?"

Druv, "As an example, I'm interested in the company's focus on innovation. I'm always looking for opportunities to learn and grow, and I think this company would provide me with that chance."

Dayita, "Excellent. Connecting your skills and experience to the company's goals and needs is also essential. How would you do that, Inaya?"

Inaya, Ok. As a software developer, I know the company is looking for someone who can contribute to its technology initiatives. I have experience developing software and working on complex projects, which I believe will be a valuable asset to the company."

Dayita, "Precisely. Finally, it's crucial to emphasize your long-term career goals and how working for the company would help you achieve them. Sameer, can you give an example?"

Sameer, "Sure. I'm interested in a career in sales, and I believe that this company's reputation for excellence in sales would provide me with an excellent foundation for my future career."

Dayita, "Perfect. Remember, when answering this question, avoiding speaking negatively about your current employer or position is crucial. Instead, focus on the positive reasons you're interested in the new position and the company. Do you all feel confident in answering this question now?"
Inaya, "It's much clearer now."

Dayita, the HR Head, sat at the head of the table, with Aarvi, Inaya, Druv, and Sameer seated across from her. They were all nervous but excited to learn from one of the top HR executives. Victor, meanwhile, was talking to someone over the phone.

Dayita smiled warmly at the candidates and said, " One of the questions that will undoubtedly come up in your interviews is, 'What are your strengths?'"

She paused for a moment to let that sink in, then continued. "This is a classic interview question that is asked to help us get a better sense of your skills and abilities. And I want to give you some tips on answering this question effectively."

"Firstly, it's important to prepare ahead of time. Take some time to think about your strengths and prepare a few examples to share. Think about your skills or qualities that make you a strong candidate for the position."

"Secondly, when discussing your strengths, try to be as specific as possible. Use examples to demonstrate your skills and abilities, and provide specific instances where you've used those strengths to achieve results."

"Thirdly, tailor your strengths to the job. When discussing your strengths, ensure they're relevant to the position you're applying for. If the job requires strong organizational skills, for example, highlight your experience with project management or other tasks that required attention to detail."

"Fourthly, it's important to avoid using cliches. Generic phrases like 'I'm a team player' or 'I'm a hard worker' don't provide much insight into your strengths. Instead, provide more specific and meaningful examples of your strengths."

"And finally, emphasize how your strengths can benefit the company. Tune your strengths to the job and explain how they can benefit the company. For example, suppose the job requires strong leadership skills. In that case, you might talk about how you've successfully led teams and how that experience could be an asset to the company."

Dayita paused, looking at each of the students in turn. " What are your strengths?' is an opportunity to showcase your skills and abilities to the interviewer. You can make a positive impression and boost your chances of obtaining the job by preparing, being specific, customizing your strengths to the job, avoiding cliches, and emphasizing how your strengths may help the firm."

She smiled again, hoping her advice would be helpful for the candidates. "Now, does anyone have any questions?"

Druv was quick to interrupt, " Then how about Weakness?"

"Alright, now it's a tricky question," Dayita said. "Well, I will ask you to tell me about your weaknesses. I know this can be a difficult question, but it's important. It's an opportunity to demonstrate self-awareness and a willingness to improve."

Aarvi, the first candidate, sat up straight and listened carefully. "Well, I'd say that one of my weaknesses is that I can be overly detail-oriented," she said. "While paying attention to details is important, I've realized that it can sometimes slow me down and prevent me from seeing the bigger picture. So, I've started delegating tasks to other team members to help me focus on the big picture and achieve our goals more efficiently."

Inaya, the second candidate, nodded her head in agreement. "I would say my weakness is my tendency to procrastinate," she said. "But I've learned to set strict deadlines and stick to them, which has helped me become more productive and efficient."

Druv, the third candidate, took a deep breath before speaking. "I must admit, I struggle with public speaking," he said. "However, I've been taking public speaking classes and practicing in front of friends and family to overcome this fear. I know it's an important skill in this role, and I'm committed to improving."

Sameer, the final candidate, smiled before responding. "I think my biggest weakness is that I can be too hard on myself," he said. "I'm a perfectionist; sometimes, it's difficult to recognize when something is good enough. But, I've started to remind myself that perfection is not always necessary and that sometimes done is better than perfect."

Dayita listened attentively to each candidate's response, impressed with their self-awareness and willingness to improve. "Thank you all for your honesty," she said. "Remember, we all have weaknesses, but how we address them matters. You've all provided examples of actively overcoming your weaknesses, which is a great sign of your dedication and commitment to self-improvement."

"It's important to show that you are aware of your weaknesses and actively working to improve them," Dayita said with a smile. "Does anyone else have any thoughts or questions about this topic?"

Druv spoke up. "I always struggle with this question. I don't want to make myself look bad, but I don't want to lie. How can I strike a balance?"

"That's a good question, Druv," Dayita replied. "It's important to be honest when discussing your weaknesses, but you also want to frame them in a positive light. Think about how you're actively working to overcome the weakness and what steps you're taking to improve."

Sameer nodded in agreement. "I think it's also important to choose a weakness that is not critical to the job you're applying for. You don't want to give the impression that you cannot perform the required tasks."

"Exactly, Sameer," Dayita said. "Choose a relevant but not critical weakness to the job, and make sure to end positively. Discuss how you're committed to self-improvement and working to overcome your weakness."

Aarvi added, "I think it's also helpful to provide specific examples of how you're addressing your weakness. It shows that you're taking concrete steps to improve and not just paying lip service to the idea of self-improvement."

Dayita smiled at Aarvi's insight. "That's a great point, Aarvi. Providing specific examples can demonstrate your dedication and commitment to self-improvement."

Dayita summarized the tips for answering the question "What are your weaknesses?" effectively, "Choose a relevant weakness, be honest, provide examples of how you're addressing the weakness, avoid critical weaknesses, and end on a positive note. By following these tips, you can answer this question effectively and make a strong impression on the interviewer."

Aarvi suddenly shifted to another topic, "I get nervous when they ask me about my career goals. I always feel like I don't have a clear plan."

Inaya nodded in agreement, "Same here. I never know how to answer that question."

Druv said, "I feel like I sound too ambitious and unrealistic when discussing my goals."

Sameer added, "I worry that my goals won't align with the company's goals, and I won't be a good fit for the position."

Dayita listened intently and then offered her advice: "Where do you see yourself in five years?' is a common interview question that is asked to assess your career goals and ambitions. Here are some tips on how to answer this question effectively."

"First, show that you have a plan. The interviewer wants to know that you have thought about your future and have a plan in place. Be specific about your goals and how you plan to achieve them. This demonstrates that you are proactive and have a clear direction. Then align your answer with the company's goals. Research the company and its goals, and align your answer with its mission and values. Show how your career goals align with the company's goals and how you plan to contribute to their success. While it's essential to demonstrate ambition, it's also important to be realistic. Avoid making unrealistic claims or setting unattainable goals. Instead, focus on how you plan to develop your skills and take on new responsibilities over the next five years. Also, remember to be open to the possibility that your career goals may change over time. Show that you are flexible and willing to adapt to new opportunities and challenges that may arise.

Finally, show enthusiasm and passion for the job and the company. This demonstrates that you are genuinely interested in the position and are committed to its success."

After the explanation, Dayita asked the group if they had any questions or concerns.

Aarvi asked, "What if I don't know what I want to do in five years?"

Dayita replied, "It's ok if your goals are not set. The important thing is to show that you have a plan and have thought about your future. You can talk about how you plan to develop your skills and take on new responsibilities over the next five years."

Inaya asked, "What if my career goals don't align with the company's goals?"

Dayita said, "It's important to research the company and its goals beforehand. Find common ground and show how your career goals can contribute to the company's success. If there are no commonalities, then it may not be the right fit for you."

Druv asked, "What if my goals are too ambitious or unrealistic?"

Dayita advised, "While it's important to demonstrate ambition, it's also important to be realistic. Avoid making unrealistic claims or setting unattainable goals. Instead, focus on how you plan to develop your skills and take on new responsibilities over the next five years."

Sameer asked, "What if I change my mind about my career goals in the future?"

Dayita responded, "Be open to the possibility that your career goals may change over time. Show that you are flexible and willing to adapt to new opportunities and challenges that may arise."

As the mentorship session ended, Dayita emphasized the importance of being enthusiastic and passionate about the job and the company during an interview. "Remember, the question 'Where do you see yourself in five years?' is an opportunity to demonstrate your ambition, career goals, and alignment with the company's goals. You can effectively answer this question and make a positive impression on the interviewer by demonstrating a strategy, matching your answer with the company's goals, being practical and flexible, and displaying passion."

Victor sat in the cafeteria, looking around at the bright, eager faces of Aarvi, Inaya, Druv, and Sameer. He couldn't help but feel proud of the opportunity he had provided them. Dayita, the HR Head of a reputed automobile company, had come in to mentor them about interview preparation. The students were soaking up her words like sponges.

As they listened intently, Victor couldn't help but feel grateful that he had met Dayita at a business conference a few years ago. They had hit it off instantly; he knew she was the perfect person to guide these young minds toward their career goals.

The conversation flowed as Dayita shared tips on answering common interview questions. She stressed the importance of showing a clear direction and aligning career goals with the company's goals. She also reminded the students to be realistic, flexible, and enthusiastic in their approach.

Victor watched as the students asked questions and engaged in meaningful discussions with Dayita. He was impressed with their eagerness to learn and take the next step in their careers. It was evident that Dayita had made a lasting impact on them.

As the session ended, Victor thanked Dayita for her time and expertise. She had been a fantastic mentor, and he knew the students had gained invaluable insights. He could already see the excitement in their eyes as they talked about the steps they would take to land their dream jobs.

As they walked out of the cafeteria, Victor couldn't help but feel a sense of pride. He had given these young minds a valuable opportunity, and he knew they would remember it for years. He was confident that they would achieve their career goals in the coming months and thanked him and Dayita for helping them get there.

Victor, "That was an amazing session, Dayita. You have a talent for mentoring young minds."

Dayita, "Thank you, Victor. You know me well. It's always a pleasure to share my knowledge and experience with these bright young students."

"Come, let's move and continue our discussion on the way"

Understanding company policies, benefits, and compensation

Victor stood at the front of the lecture hall, eagerly awaiting the arrival of his students. He had been counting the days until this final lecture on "Understanding Corporate Companies." He had a surprise in store for his pupils.

As the students filed in, Victor greeted them warmly, "Good morning, everyone! How are you all doing today?"

The students replied with a mix of groans and grumbles, still trying to shake off the sleepiness from their early morning classes.

Victor chuckled, "Well, I promise to make this lecture worth your while. Today, we will dive into the fascinating world of corporate structures."

The students perked up, curious about what Victor had in store for them.
"So, let's start with the basics," Victor began. "What are the different types of corporate structures?"

A student raised her hand, "Is it like LLC, Pvt. Ltd., and Public Limited?"

Victor nodded, "Yes, exactly. You guys have done your research, I see. So, we have LLC, Pvt. Ltd., Public Limited, and more. Each has its benefits and drawbacks, and it's important to understand them before deciding which structure is right for you."

The students nodded in agreement, scribbling notes in their notebooks.

"Moving on," Victor continued, "let's talk about the pros and cons of working for a large corporation versus a small business."

A student raised her hand again, "Which one do you prefer, Victor?"

Victor grinned, "Ah, I can't reveal that just yet. But what I can tell you is that both have their perks. Large corporations offer job stability and opportunities for growth. At the same time, small businesses allow for a more intimate work environment and the chance to wear many hats."
The students nodded, jotting down notes as Victor continued to speak.

Finally, the lecture drew close, and Victor approached Aarvi, Inaya, Druv, and Sameer, who was sitting near the front.

"So, what did you all think?" he asked, smiling.

Aarvi spoke up first. "It was exciting, but I wish we had more time to learn about the different departments within a corporation."

Inaya nodded in agreement. "Yeah, and it would have been cool to hear about corporate challenges."

Druv chimed in. "I liked learning about the different types of corporate structures, but I'm curious about how companies decide which one to use."

Sameer added, "I thought it was great overall, but I wish we had more real-life examples to help us understand the concepts better."

Victor listened to their feedback and then grinned. "Well, I have some good news for you all. I have one more surprise in store."

The students looked at each other, curious. "What is it?" they asked eagerly.

"You will get to know about it. I've arranged for you all transportation," Victor said. "The surprise awaited you at one of the fastest-growing Biotech companies in the city."

The students' faces lit up with excitement. "That's amazing!" Aarvi exclaimed.
"I can't wait!" Inaya said, bouncing in her seat.
Druv and Sameer high-fived each other, grinning from ear to ear.

Victor smiled at their enthusiasm. "I'm glad you all are excited. It's going to be a great learning experience."

The students thanked him profusely, and as they filed out of the lecture hall, they chattered excitedly about their upcoming visit. Victor watched them go, feeling happy he could give them this opportunity to learn more about corporate companies.

Aarvi, Inaya, Druv, and Sameer were excited as they followed Victor to the office of the fast-moving Biotech Startup in Bengaluru. They were curious to see what awaited them.

They were greeted by a tall man with a friendly smile as they entered the office. "Welcome, everyone! I'm Neel Sarin, the founder of this startup. It's great to have you all here."

The students shook his hand, introducing themselves. They were impressed by the modern, sleek office and the buzzing energy in the air.

As they chatted with Neel, they noticed another woman walking towards them. "Hey, everyone! I'm Shivani Mitra, the HR head at Victor's tech company. I came from our Delhi office to be here today," she said, smiling warmly.

The students were surprised and impressed by Shivani's dedication. They greeted her and thanked her for taking the time to join them.

As a final and familiar surprise, Dayita entered the Hall. Her heels clicked on the polished floor, drawing everyone's attention. All eyes were on her as she strode purposefully towards her office, her sharp business suit and sleek hair making her look like a force to be reckoned with. She smiled and greeted everyone and straight away sat near Victor.

The room was filled with excitement as the students settled into their seats. They had been eagerly waiting for this fireside chat with Dayita, Neel, and Shivani, hoping to better understand corporate life.

Dayita, Neel, and Shivani looked like the perfect team as they took their places in front of the students. Dayita was dressed in a sharp business suit, exuding confidence and authority. Neel looked casual yet professional in his crisp shirt and jeans. Shivani had a warm smile on her face that immediately put everyone at ease.

"Good evening, everyone," Dayita began. "We're here to talk about important topics that we know are on your mind. We'll be discussing company policies, benefits, and compensation."

Dayita, the Chief Human Resource Officer of a leading MNC, started by giving an overview of company policies. She explained, "As you embark on your new job, it's important to understand the various aspects of your employment, from company policies to benefits and compensation."

She paused and said, "Let's talk about company policies. Understanding company policies is an important aspect of starting a new job. These policies can cover various topics, from expected behavior in the workplace to attendance requirements and leave policies. We will explore some real-life examples of company policies to give you a better idea of what you might encounter in your new job."

"Let's start with dress codes. Many companies have policies that dictate what employees should wear to work. For example, some companies require business attire, while others allow casual dress. Some companies might have specific dress codes for different departments or job roles. It's important to understand your company's dress code policy and follow it to the letter to ensure you present a professional image."

She moved to another example, "Another example of a company policy is attendance requirements. Most companies have policies that dictate how often employees can miss work without penalty. Some companies might require that employees provide a doctor's note for absences due to illness. In contrast, others might allow several sick days per year. Understanding your company's attendance policy is crucial to avoid misunderstandings and ensure you meet your employer's expectations."

She came to another topic and, with a severe tone, continued, "Many companies offer paid time off for vacations, holidays, and personal days. Understanding your company's leave policy is critical to ensuring you take advantage of these benefits while fulfilling your job responsibilities. Some companies might have specific requirements for requesting time off, such as submitting a request several days in advance. Others might have blackout dates where time off is not allowed due to busy periods."

"Understanding your company's policies is essential to your success as an employee. Reviewing these policies and asking questions when necessary can help you avoid misunderstandings and ensure that you're meeting your employer's expectations. By doing so, you can focus on your job and contribute to your company's success."

Next up was Neel, who spoke about the benefits that companies offer their employees. He explained in a sharp voice, "These are the perks that come with your job, such as health insurance, retirement plans, and paid time off. Understanding company benefits is an important aspect of starting a new job. These benefits can be critical to your overall job satisfaction and financial well-being. Let us explore some real-life examples of common company benefits to give you a better idea of what you might expect."

"One of the most common company benefits is health insurance. Many companies offer health insurance plans to help employees manage their healthcare costs. These plans might include coverage for medical, dental, and vision expenses. It's important to understand what your health insurance plan covers, how to enroll, and how to file claims. For example, some plans might require you to select a primary care physician or obtain a referral to see a specialist."

He leaned towards the students and continued, "For instance, let's say you work for a tech startup that offers health insurance benefits. Your employer might offer various plan options with different coverage levels and premiums. You must review each plan carefully to determine which best meets your needs. Once you've selected a plan, you must enroll during the company's open enrollment period. After you're enrolled, you'll receive a health insurance card that you can use to access medical care."

"Retirement plans are another common company benefit. These plans can help employees save for retirement and provide a source of income once they stop working. One common type of retirement plan is a 401(k) plan. With a 401(k) plan, employees can contribute a portion of their pre-tax income to the plan, which is then invested in various funds. Some companies might also offer matching contributions, which means they will contribute a certain amount to the plan on the employee's behalf."

He elaborated with an example, "Let's say you work for a large corporation that offers a 401(k) plan. You'll need to review the plan's investment options to determine how you want your contributions to be invested. Some plans might offer a mix of stocks, bonds, and mutual funds, while others might focus on a specific type of investment. You'll also need to decide how much to contribute to the plan each pay period. Many financial experts recommend contributing at least enough to maximize employer matching contributions."

"Paid time off is another important company benefit. This benefit typically includes vacation time, sick days, and personal days. It's important to understand how much time off you're entitled to and how to request it. For example, some companies might require that you request time off a certain number of days in advance, while others might have blackout dates where time off is not allowed."

He pointed to Aarvi and said, "For instance, let's say you work for a retail chain that offers paid time off benefits. You'll need to review the company's policy to determine how much time off you're entitled to and how to request it. You might be able to accrue a certain number of vacation days each year based on your length of service with the company. You'll also need to follow the company's procedures for requesting time off, such as submitting a request to your supervisor a certain number of days in advance."

He wrapped up and said, "Understanding your company's benefits is critical to making the most of your employment. By reviewing these benefits and asking questions when necessary, you can ensure that you're taking advantage of everything your company has to offer. Whether it's health insurance, retirement plans, or paid time off, these benefits can significantly improve your overall job satisfaction and financial well-being."

Now it was Shivani's turn to explain the different types of compensation that employees receive, including base pay, bonuses, and stock options. She was also to discuss the importance of negotiating for better compensation and to provide tips on how to do it effectively.

Shivani said, "One of the most critical aspects of your employment is your compensation. Your compensation package is one of the most important aspects of your employment, as it determines how much money you'll earn and what other benefits you'll receive. Negotiating a fair compensation package can be challenging. Still, it's essential to ensure that you're being paid what you're worth and that you're satisfied with the terms of your employment."

She had a pleasant voice. She smiled and said, "One of the best ways to negotiate a fair compensation package is to research salaries for similar positions in your industry and geographic area. This can help you understand the going rate for your experience and qualifications and give you a benchmark to use when negotiating with your employer. For example, suppose you're applying for a job as a software engineer in New York City. In that case, you might research what other software engineers in the area are earning and use this information to inform your negotiations."

"Preparing a strong case for why you deserve a certain level of compensation is also critical. This can involve highlighting your experience, qualifications, and accomplishments and explaining how you can add value to the company. For example, emphasize these points throughout your talks if you've led successful projects, gotten praises from past companies, or have a unique skill set that sets you apart from other candidates."

She adjusted her position and continued, "Being prepared to negotiate is also essential. Negotiating your compensation package can be uncomfortable, but it's important to advocate for yourself and be clear about what you want. This can involve asking for a higher salary, additional benefits, or other forms of compensation. For example, suppose you're negotiating a job offer with a lower salary than you were hoping for. In that case, you might ask if there's room for negotiation or if other benefits could be included in the package."

"Real-life examples of successful negotiations can be helpful when preparing to negotiate your compensation package. For instance, a recent survey by Glassdoor found that 59% of workers who negotiated their salaries received higher pay. This demonstrates that negotiation can be a powerful tool for ensuring fair compensation."

She explained further, "Another example might be an individual who was offered a job with a starting salary of $60,000 per year. After researching salaries for similar positions and preparing a strong case for why they were worth more, they negotiated a salary of $70,000 per year. This 16.7% increase in salary can make a significant difference in their overall financial well-being."

Finally, she said, "Negotiating a fair compensation package is critical to ensuring your financial well-being and job satisfaction. You can ensure that you're being paid what you're worth and that you're content with the terms of your work by studying salaries, developing a compelling case for why you're worth a given remuneration, and being prepared to negotiate. Don't be afraid to advocate for yourself and ask for your worth – it can make a significant difference in your career and life."

Aarvi, "That sounds interesting, Shivani. Can you tell us more about how salaries are determined and whether they're negotiable?"

Shivani, "Sure, Aarvi. Salaries can vary depending on the company and the job you're applying for. Some companies might have a salary range for a particular job. In contrast, others might be open to negotiation based on your experience and qualifications. For example, suppose you have a strong track record in the industry and can demonstrate how you can add value to the company. In that case, you might be able to negotiate a higher salary."

Druv, "What about bonuses? Are those a common form of compensation?"

Shivani, "Absolutely, Druv. Bonuses are another common form of compensation, typically given based on performance. These can be one-time payments, such as a meeting or exceeding sales goals or completing a project on time and under budget. Some companies might offer bonuses regularly, such as quarterly or annually. In contrast, others might offer them as a one-time reward for a specific achievement."

Sameer, "What about stock options? Are those only for certain industries?"

Shivani, "No, Sameer, stock options can be a common form of compensation in many industries, but they're prevalent in the tech industry. These contracts allow you to buy company stock at a certain price, usually lower than the current market price. Suppose the company performs well and the stock price rises over time. In that case, you can exercise your option and purchase the shares at a lower price before selling them on the market for a profit."

Inaya, "What other forms of compensation are there?"

Shivani, "Other forms of compensation might include profit-sharing plans, which give you a share of the company's profits based on your role and performance, or commission-based pay, which is common in sales roles and pays you a percentage the revenue you generate. Understanding your company's compensation packages is critical to maximizing your employment. By reviewing these packages and asking questions when necessary, you can ensure that you're receiving fair compensation for your work. It's important to understand the details of each package and how to make the most of them to ensure your success as an employee."
Druv, "Thanks, Shivani. This was helpful."

Sameer, "Yeah, I feel a lot more informed. Thanks to all of you for such a wonderful session."

All four of them nodded together.

Dayita, Neel, and Shivani smiled and looked at Victor, who was profoundly thinking.

As the chat ended, the students thanked Dayita, Neel, and Shivani for their time and insights. They had learned so much about the corporate world and how it operated.

As they left the office, Aarvi turned to Victor. "Thank you so much for arranging this visit, Victor. It was an amazing experience."

Inaya nodded in agreement. "Yeah, we learned so much. It was eye-opening."
Druv added, "I'm so grateful for this opportunity. It was cool to learn everything from the best."
Sameer smiled. "And meeting Neel and Shivani was amazing. They were so friendly and helpful."

Victor beamed with pride. "I'm glad you all enjoyed it. This is just the beginning of your journey in corporate companies."

As the fireside chat ended, the students reluctantly filed out of the conference room, their minds buzzing with all the new knowledge they had gained about company policies, benefits, and compensation.

Victor Edmund approached Aarvi, Inaya, Druv, and Sameer, a bittersweet expression on his face. "Well, that's it for me," he said, his voice tinged with sadness. "I'm leaving for London tomorrow morning."

The students looked at each other, a mix of emotions evident on their faces. They were sad to see Victor go but excited to put their newly acquired knowledge into practice. "Thank you so much for everything, Victor," Aarvi said, her voice filled with gratitude. "We've learned so much from you."

Victor smiled warmly at her. "It's been my pleasure, Aarvi. I do not doubt that you and your classmates will go on to do great things in the corporate world."

Inaya, Druv, and Sameer agreed, thanking Victor for his guidance and support over the past few months.

As Victor exited the conference room, the students couldn't help but feel a twinge of sadness. But they knew their lessons from him would stay with them for a lifetime, and they were excited to see where their newfound knowledge would take them.

The Break

Aarvi, Inaya, Druv, and Sameer at B-School were excited after attending the lectures and first-hand experience from the world's top tech company CEO. Victor's insights and knowledge inspired the students to think beyond the boundaries of their textbooks and assignments. They were driven to impact the industry and change the world. However, as time passed, the students gradually returned to their usual routine of assignments, tests, and regular activities. And Aarvi, Inaya, Druv, and Sameer were consumed with deadlines, exams, and projects.

One day, as the students were going about their usual routine, the Dean of the B-School called them to his office. Aarvi, Druv, Sameer, and Inaya walked into the Dean's office, wondering what the meeting could be about. The Dean informed them that they had received an official letter from Victor's office, offering internships to all four of them in the London office for six months. The students were stunned. This was a once-in-a-lifetime opportunity, and they couldn't believe it was happening to them.

The news of the internships rekindled the students' motivation and drive. They immediately prepared for the internship, determined to make the most of this incredible opportunity.

The students were greeted with excitement and anticipation as they landed in London. The city was alive with energy and innovation, and the Victor office was a hub of creativity and inspiration.

Aarvi, Inaya, Druv, and Sameer were all students at a prestigious B-School in Bengaluru, India. They had been eagerly anticipating their trip to London, where they would be the first meeting with the HR team at Victor's office as instructed. When they arrived, they were greeted by a friendly face - Shivani, who had flown in from the New Delhi office for an HR conclave.

Shivani wasted no time introducing the students to the rest of the HR team. She was warm and friendly and made them feel at ease right away. As they settled in, Shivani began to explain what they could expect from an internship in London.

"London is the biggest city in Europe," she said, "and a hub for creativity, productivity, and culture. This means that London has an incredible range of placement options for internship-seekers. You'll find opportunities to gain valuable experience in business, government, or entertainment, to name a few."

The students listened attentively, eager to learn more. Shivani explained that most of London's interns were recent graduates and that it was essential to start planning if they wanted to make the most of their time in the city.
"London is more expensive than most U.S. cities, especially during the summer," she said. "But we've arranged approved accommodation for you, so you don't have to worry about that."

Shivani also emphasized the importance of professionalism in the workplace. "No matter where in the world you're working, it's a good idea to be as professional as possible, prompt, and respectful of others," she said. "London is no exception, but there are a few differences to expect. Personal space is important to Brits, so handshakes are normal, but hugs and friendly kisses can be a bit much in the workplace."

The students nodded in agreement, taking note of Shivani's advice. They were excited about their internship in London and grateful for the opportunity to learn from such an experienced HR team. With Shivani's guidance, they knew they could become better interns and take their careers to the next level.

Making a Smooth Transition into the New Role

The next day, Aarvi, Druv, Inaya, and Sammer, four interns from B-School, Bengaluru, arrived at the doorstep of Victor's Tech Firm. The excitement in the air was palpable as they made their way inside, taking in the sleek modern design of the reception area.

As they approached the reception desk, they were greeted by a friendly face who welcomed them to the company and asked for their names. After confirming their identities, they were given their access cards and escorted to the elevators by the receptionist.

The ride up to the 10th floor was filled with nervous chatter as they discussed what they expected from their first day. They all knew this was a fantastic opportunity to learn from some of the best minds in the tech industry and were determined to make the most of it.

As they exited the elevator and made their way to the intern area, they were greeted by rows upon rows of desks, each occupied by a bright-eyed and bushy-tailed intern. The atmosphere was electric, with keyboards clicking and the occasional laughter as someone cracked a joke.

Aarvi, Druv, Inaya, and Sammer found their seats and settled in, taking in the surroundings and preparing for the day ahead. Just then, a tall, imposing figure strode into the room, and the interns all fell silent.

Mr. Victor, the company's CEO, was present. He greeted the interns and gave them an overview of what they should expect during their time with the organization. Victor highlighted the value of hard work, devotion, and collaboration. He encouraged them to make the most of their time at Victor.

With that, he left the room, and the interns were left to start their day. Aarvi, Druv, Inaya, and Sammer felt slightly disappointed as Victor's face was not friendly as they had seen previously. As Victor opened the door to step out, he just turned back and smiled at their favorite interns. He then instructed his assistant to arrange a debriefing session for the new interns.

Shivani was waiting for them and two colleagues in a small conference room at the corner of the 10th floor.

Shivani made them feel at ease as she knew how tensed these freshers may be.

She said, "Hi Aarvi, Druv, Inaya, and Sammer. Today, I want to talk to you about starting a new job or transitioning into a new role. It can be a daunting experience, but with the right mindset and approach, you can make a smooth transition and excel in your new role.

One of the most important things you need to do when starting a new job is to build relationships with your colleagues. It would help if you established trust and rapport with them so that you can work effectively as a team. One way to do this is by being approachable and friendly. When you meet your colleagues, introduce yourself, ask questions, and show a genuine interest in getting to know them. Remember that everyone was new once, and people are usually more than happy to help out a new team member.

Another way to build relationships with your colleagues is by participating in team-building activities. These activities can range from social outings to team-building exercises. They allow you to bond with and get to know your colleagues outside the workplace. Participating in team-building activities will develop a sense of camaraderie and establish a strong foundation for working together as a team.

So, Aarvi, Druv, Inaya, and Sammer, always remember to be approachable and friendly and participate in team-building activities to build strong relationships with your colleagues. It will help you transition smoothly and excel in your new role. Do you have any questions or thoughts about this?"

Aarvi, "Can you explain a few specific examples of team-building activities I could use?"

Shivani, "Of course, Aarvi. There are many different types of team-building activities that you could suggest to your new team. Some examples include:
- Volunteering for a local charity or community project
- Organizing a team lunch or happy hour
- Participating in a sports league or fitness challenge
- Attending a team-building workshop or seminar

- Planning a team outing to a local attraction or event

These are just a few examples, but the possibilities are endless. The key is to find an activity that everyone is interested in and allows you to bond and get to know each other better."

Druv, "That sounds great. Do you have any tips for building workplace relationships with colleagues?"

Shivani," Definitely, Druv. One way to build relationships with your colleagues during work hours is by offering to help them with their work. If you notice a colleague struggling with a task, offer to lend a hand. This will show that you're a team player and allow you to work closely with your colleague and learn more about their strengths and weaknesses."

Inaya, "Those are great tips. Do you have any advice for getting to know colleagues who have been with the company long?"

Shivani, "That's a great question, Inaya. One way to get to know colleagues who have been with the company for a long time is by asking them about their experiences and how they've seen the company change over the years. People love to share their stories, and by listening to their experiences, you'll better understand the company culture and history."

Shivani, "Another important aspect of starting a new job is asking for help. It's important to remember that no one knows everything, and it's okay to ask for help when you need it. Asking for help shows you're committed to learning and growing in your new role. When you ask for help, be specific about what you need help with and who can provide the assistance you need. This will ensure you receive the right support and avoid wasting time."

Sameer, "That's great advice. Do you have any tips on finding a mentor?"

Shivani, "Absolutely, Sameer. Finding a mentor can be a great way to get guidance and support as you navigate your new role. When looking for a mentor, choose someone you trust and respect and who has experience in your field or company. Choosing someone with the time and willingness to support you is also important. Don't be afraid to reach out to people who you think would be a good fit as a mentor and ask if they're willing to meet with you."

Druv, "That sounds like a great idea. Are there any other benefits to having a mentor?"

Shivani, "Definitely, Druv. In addition to providing guidance and support, a mentor can help you navigate the company culture and establish relationships with key stakeholders. They can also provide valuable feedback on your work and help you identify areas for improvement."

Inaya, "That sounds helpful. Do you have any advice on approaching a mentor for guidance?"

Shivani, "Of course, Inaya. When approaching a mentor, be respectful of their time and come prepared with specific questions or challenges you're facing. It's also important to be open to their feedback and suggestions, even if it's not what you want to hear."

Shivani, "Adjusting to a new work environment can be tough, but it's important to approach it with an open mind. One way to do this is by familiarizing yourself with the company culture and values. Understanding the culture and values will help you understand what's expected of you in the workplace and help you build relationships with your colleagues."

Sammer, "That makes sense. How do we go about learning the company culture and values?"

Shivani, "Great question, Sameer. You can learn about the company culture and values by observing how people interact with each other and the company's policies and practices. You can also ask your colleagues or the HR department about the company's mission, vision, and values. Understanding the company's culture and values will make you better equipped to fit in and contribute to the workplace. It's common to encounter different systems and processes when starting a new job. The best approach is to be open-minded and willing to learn new working methods. Don't be afraid to ask questions and seek guidance from your colleagues or supervisor. By being flexible and adaptable, you'll be able to integrate into the new work environment more quickly and effectively."

Inaya, "That's helpful. Can we do anything else to adjust to a new work environment?"

Shivani, "Yes, Inaya. It's important to remember that building relationships with your colleagues is critical to succeeding in your new role. Be friendly and approachable, and take the initiative to get to know your colleagues. Also, ask for feedback on your work and be open to constructive criticism. By doing this, you'll be able to learn from your mistakes and improve your performance."

Everyone thanked Shivani for her helpful and valuable advice, which made them feel more confident about starting their internship.

Shivani concluded, "Remember, adjusting to a new work environment takes time, but by being open-minded and building relationships with your colleagues, you'll be able to adapt more quickly and effectively.

A smooth transition into a new role is essential for success and job satisfaction. Building relationships with colleagues, asking for help, and adjusting to the new work environment are crucial aspects of a successful transition. You can build strong relationships with colleagues by being approachable, participating in team-building activities, and seeking out a mentor. You can receive the right kind of support by being specific when asking for help and seeking out a mentor. By familiarizing yourself with the company culture and being open to new ways of doing things, you can adjust to the new work environment more quickly and effectively.

Remember, making a successful transition takes time and effort, so be patient with yourself and trust the process. It's natural to feel overwhelmed and unsure at first. Still, you can overcome challenges and excel in your new role with persistence and dedication.

It's also important to remember that every transition is unique. What works for one person may not work for another. Therefore, it's crucial to approach the transition process with an open mind and a willingness to experiment with different strategies.

Finally, don't be afraid to celebrate your successes along the way, no matter how small they may seem. Celebrating your progress and accomplishments will help you stay motivated and focused on achieving your goals.

In conclusion, smoothly transitioning into a new role requires effort, patience, and a willingness to learn and adapt. You can successfully transition and thrive in your new role by building solid relationships with colleagues, asking for help when needed, and adjusting to the new work environment. Remember to approach the transition process with an open mind and celebrate your successes."

"Good luck!"

As they returned to their desks, Aarvi, Druv, Inaya, and Sameer felt more confident and prepared to take on their new roles. They were grateful for Shivani's mentoring and guidance, which helped them navigate the challenges of starting a new job or transitioning into a new role. With a better understanding of the company's culture and values, a strong network of colleagues and mentors, and an open-minded and adaptable approach, they were ready to tackle their assigned jobs enthusiastically and optimistically. As they sat at their desks, they felt a sense of accomplishment and satisfaction, knowing they had taken an important step towards a successful career.

Time management and productivity tips

Aarvi, Druv, Inaya, and Sameer had always dreamt of working in a tech company. So when they received their acceptance letter for an internship at a top tech company in London, they were overjoyed. They couldn't wait to experience a corporate employee's fast-paced and exciting life.

However, as the days passed, they soon realized that corporate life was not what they had imagined. The workload was overwhelming, and the pressure to meet deadlines was immense. They barely had any time to rest or care for themselves, and it wasn't long before their health began to suffer.

Victor, the CEO of the tech company, had been watching the interns closely. Although he was pleased with their performance, he saw they were struggling. He knew that he needed to step in and offer some guidance.

One morning, Victor summoned the interns for a discussion during his morning walk at a nearby park. Aarvi, Druv, Inaya, and Sameer were nervous as they made their way to the park, knowing they had fallen short of expectations.

As they arrived, they saw Victor sitting on a bench, already finished with his walk. They quickly apologized for being late, but Victor waved it off and motioned for them to sit beside him.

"Tell me, how are you all doing?" Victor asked, his tone gentle but firm.

Aarvi, Druv, Inaya, and Sameer looked at each other, unsure where to begin. Finally, Aarvi spoke up. "We're finding it hard to keep up with everything," she admitted. "There's just so much to do, and we don't know how to manage our time."

Victor nodded thoughtfully. "I understand," he said. "Corporate life can be overwhelming, especially for new interns. But I want you all to know you can come to me anytime for guidance. I've been in your shoes before and know how hard it can be."

"Alright, guys, let's get started," Victor said, leaning back on his bench. "Today, we will talk about time management and productivity."

Sameer raised his hand, " I'm always running out of time, and my to-do list keeps getting longer. How can I manage my time better?"

Victor smiled, "Great question, Sameer. The first thing you need to do is prioritize your tasks. You can't do everything all at once, so you need to identify the most important tasks and focus on them first."

Druv nodded in agreement, "But how do we determine which tasks are the most important?"

Victor leaned forward, "You need to consider three factors when prioritizing your tasks: importance, urgency, and impact. Which tasks are the most important to your work or personal life? Which tasks have a deadline or require immediate attention? And which tasks have the most significant impact on your goals or well-being?"

Aarvi said, "What about large tasks that seem impossible to complete?"

Victor chuckled, "Breaking down large tasks into smaller, manageable tasks is a great way to tackle them. You can then prioritize these smaller tasks based on their importance and urgency."

"But what if I'm interrupted by emails or phone calls while attempting to focus on a task?" Inaya frowned.

Victor nodded, "That's where time-blocking comes in. Set aside specific blocks of time for your most important tasks and minimize interruptions during those blocks. You can also batch similar tasks together to improve efficiency."

The interns nodded, eager to implement these tips into their daily routines.

Victor continued, "Let's talk about setting goals. Who can tell me what a specific goal is?"
Sameer eagerly raised his hand. "A specific goal is clearly defined, like 'launching a new product by the end of the year.'"

"Exactly!" Victor exclaimed. "Now, let's make sure your goals are achievable. Druv, can you give me an example of how to break down a big goal into smaller steps?"

Druv nodded. "Sure. Suppose my goal is to increase our social media following by 10,000 followers. In that case, I can break it down into smaller steps like creating more engaging content and running social media ads."

"Great job, Druv," Victor said. "Now, Aarvi, why is it important to align your goals with your values?"

Aarvi thought for a moment before answering. "When your goals align with your values, you're more motivated to achieve them. For example, if I value sustainability, I might aim to reduce our company's carbon footprint by 20%."

"Exactly," Victor said with a smile. "And finally, Inaya, can you tell me why writing down your goals is important?"

Inaya nodded. "Writing down your goals helps you commit to them and makes them more real. Plus, it helps you track your progress and stay motivated."

"Perfect," Victor said, impressed with his interns' understanding. "Now, let's each take a few minutes to write down three specific, achievable, and aligned goals. Then, we'll share them with the group and discuss how we can support each other in achieving them."

The interns got to work, scribbling down their goals on notepads. Victor could feel the energy and excitement building as they shared their goals with the group. He knew that these interns would accomplish great things with some guidance and support.

Victor summarized the discussion, "Setting goals is an essential part of achieving success in any area of life. By setting specific, achievable goals that align with your values and priorities, you can focus your efforts and resources, track your progress, and measure your success. Remember, goal-setting is an ongoing process requiring commitment, effort, and flexibility to achieve the best possible outcome."

"I've been struggling to stay focused," admitted Inaya. "There are so many distractions, and I feel like I can't get anything done."

Victor nodded in understanding. "Distractions can be a challenge. Have you tried identifying what distracts you the most?"

Inaya thought for a moment before responding. "I think it's social media. I'm always checking my accounts and responding to notifications."

"Okay, that's a good start," Victor said. "You could turn off your notifications and set specific times for checking your accounts. That way, you can minimize the distractions and focus on your tasks."

Druv said, "I have trouble with my colleagues interrupting me while trying to work."

Victor nodded. "That's a common issue. Have you tried setting boundaries with your colleagues? Letting them know when you're not available for chit-chat?"

Druv nodded. "Yeah, I've started closing my office door when I need to focus, and I try to let my colleagues know when I'm working on something important."

"Great, that's a good way to set boundaries and avoid distractions," said Victor.

Aarvi spoke up next. "I have trouble with noise distracting me. There's always someone talking on the phone or typing loudly."

Victor smiled. "I can relate to that. Have you tried using noise-canceling headphones?"

Aarvi shook her head. "No, I haven't. Do you think that would help?"

"Definitely," said Victor. "Noise-cancelling headphones can block distracting sounds and help you focus on your tasks." Finally, Sameer spoke up. "I've been struggling to stay motivated. I feel like I'm not making progress on my goals."

Victor nodded. "That's understandable. It can be hard to stay motivated when you feel like you're not making progress. Have you tried taking regular breaks?"

Sameer looked surprised. "Breaks? How would that help?" "Taking regular breaks can help you stay focused and avoid distractions," explained Victor. "Breaks give your brain a chance to rest and recharge, which can improve your focus and productivity when you return to your tasks."

The interns nodded in understanding, grateful for the tips and advice from their mentor.

He began the next point of his conversation with a friendly tone, "I know that juggling work and personal life can be challenging, but it's important to find a balance that works for you."

Sameer looked overwhelmed and said, "I'm finding it hard to focus on anything other than work. I feel like I'm always working and can't find time for anything else."

Victor nodded understandingly and replied, "That's a common feeling, Sameer. It's important to set boundaries and prioritize self-care to avoid burnout. Have you considered setting specific work hours and sticking to them?"

Druv added, "I'm having trouble disconnecting from work, even when I'm not at the office."

Victor suggested, "You can avoid checking work emails or taking work calls during your time. Respecting your time and prioritizing activities that help you relax and recharge are important. What activities do you enjoy outside of work?"
Aarvi said, "I find balancing work and family responsibilities difficult."

Victor replied, "Delegating responsibilities can help you balance work and personal life. It's important to identify tasks that can be delegated to others, such as colleagues or family members, and trust them to handle those tasks effectively."

Inaya added, "I'm unsure how to balance my schedule effectively."

Victor suggested, "Being mindful of your schedule can help you balance work and personal life more effectively. It's important to be aware of how much time you spend on work-related and personal activities and make adjustments as needed. You can also take advantage of flexible work arrangements, such as telecommuting or flexible schedules."
The group nodded, feeling empowered to take control of their work and personal lives. "Thanks, Victor, for the helpful advice," they said unison.

"Okay, guys, Finally, let's talk about self-care. It's essential for your well-being, especially during this busy internship period. Who wants to share what they do for self-care?" Victor asked.

Sameer spoke up first. "I like to schedule some me-time every week. It could be anything from reading a book, watching my favorite show, or trying out a new recipe."

"Great idea, Sameer," Victor nodded. "Scheduling in self-care activities is key. Druv, what about you?"

"I practice mindfulness," Druv said. "It helps me stay centered and focused, especially when work gets overwhelming."

"That's awesome, Druv," Victor said with a smile. "Mindfulness is a great way to prioritize self-care. Aarvi, what about you?"

"I make sure to get enough sleep," Aarvi said. "I've realized that I'm not productive or focused without proper rest."

"Excellent point, Aarvi," Victor said. "Getting enough sleep is crucial. Inaya, what do you do for self-care?"

"I like to engage in physical activity," Inaya said. "I find that exercise helps me clear my mind and de-stress."

"Fantastic, Inaya," Victor said. "Exercise is a great way to improve both physical and mental health. Remember, it's important to unplug from technology too, and make time for the activities that make you feel happy and relaxed."

The interns nodded in agreement, and Victor smiled. "Good job, everyone. Don't forget to prioritize self-care, even when work gets hectic. It'll help you perform better in the long run."

"Let's Conclude." Said Victor checking his watch. "Time management and productivity are key to success in all aspects of life. By prioritizing tasks, setting goals, avoiding distractions, balancing work and personal life, and finding time for self-care, you can master your time and productivity and achieve your goals. Remember, the most successful people in the world have the same time as you. It's how you use that time that makes all the difference."

As the mentoring session ended, Victor looked at Sameer, Druv, Aarvi, and Inaya with a smile. "I hope you all found these tips helpful in mastering your time and productivity," he said. "Time is a valuable resource, and it's up to you to make the most of it."

The interns nodded in agreement, grateful for the valuable advice that Victor had shared with them. "Thank you so much for your guidance," Sameer said. "I feel much more confident about managing my time and achieving my goals now."

"Me too," added Inaya. "I can't wait to implement these tips and see the results."

"Excellent," Victor said. "I do not doubt that with these time management and productivity strategies, you can accomplish anything you want. Remember to stay focused, avoid distractions, and make time for self-care. You've got this!"

The interns said their goodbyes to Victor, feeling inspired and motivated to take charge of their time and productivity. They knew that by following these tips, they would be on the path to success.

Building relationships with colleagues

It was a bright and early morning in London, the sun shone, and the birds were chirping. Sameer, Druv, Aarvi, and Inaya, four interns at a bustling corporate office, were up and ready to start their day. They arrived at the office with a spring in their step, eager to absorb everything the corporate atmosphere offered.

As they made their way to their respective departments, they quickly realized the importance of building relationships with their colleagues. After all, their purpose in being here was to learn and develop; connecting with others is one of the best ways to achieve that.

As Sameer walked into the finance department, he noticed a group huddled around a computer screen. He made his way over to them and introduced himself. "Hey, I'm Sameer, one of the new interns. What's everyone looking at?"

One of the colleagues turned to him and smiled. "Hi Sameer, I'm Alex. We're just looking at some financial reports for the quarter. It's not the most exciting stuff, but it's important." Sameer nodded. "Yeah, I can imagine. I'm interested in learning more about finance and its workings within the company. Would you be free to chat over coffee or lunch sometime?"

Alex smiled again. "Sure thing, we'd be happy to chat with you. Let's plan on grabbing lunch together tomorrow."

As Druv made his way to the management department, he noticed his supervisor, Sarah, sitting at her desk. He approached her with a smile. "Hi Sarah, it's great to see you. I'm excited to learn more about the management side of things."

Sarah returned the smile. "Hi Druv, it's great to have you here. We have many exciting projects, and I think you'll be a great addition to the team."

Druv nodded eagerly. "I'm ready to dive in and help in any way possible. Is there anything I can assist with right now?"

Sarah looked surprised but pleased. "There is something. We're putting together a proposal for a new project, and I could use another set of eyes. Would you be interested in taking a look and offering your input?"

Druv nodded eagerly. " I'd love to help out in any way I can." As Aarvi entered the marketing department, she was greeted by a team of enthusiastic marketers. They were discussing their latest ad campaign, and Aarvi was impressed by the creativity and innovation that had gone into it.

"Hey there, I'm Aarvi," she said with a smile. "I'm one of the new interns. I just wanted to say that I love what you guys have done with the latest ad campaign. It's creative and engaging."

The team members thanked her and asked if she had any ideas to add. Aarvi nodded eagerly. " I do have a few ideas that I think could work well. Would it be okay if I shared them with you guys?"

The team members were happy to hear her ideas, and they spent the next hour brainstorming and developing new concepts. Aarvi felt energized and inspired by the collaborative process. She knew that she had found her niche within the company.

As Inaya walked around the office, she conversed with colleagues from different departments. She asked about their hobbies and interests outside of work and found that they were all passionate about different things.

One colleague, a software developer named Tom, told her about his love of photography. Another colleague, a marketing specialist, Maya, shared her passion for hiking and the outdoors. Inaya was impressed by the diversity of interests and talents within the company, and she made a mental note to continue getting to know her colleagues on a personal level.

The interns quickly learned that building colleague relationships weren't just about networking. It was about creating a sense of community within the workplace. They all felt a sense of belonging and knew that they were part of something bigger than themselves.

Impressed by their quick adaptation to the corporate world, Victor, the CEO, decided to organize a team-building event for the interns. He wanted to give them some tips at the end of the event on how to build relationships with colleagues in a fun and engaging way.

The interns were excited about the team-building event organized by Victor, the CEO. They gathered in the lobby, where Victor greeted them and explained the scavenger hunt rules. The teams were already formed, each with a mix of interns and colleagues from different departments.

"Good morning, everyone! I hope you all had a great start to your day," Victor began. "Today, we'll have some fun while learning how to build relationships with your colleagues. The scavenger hunt will help you work together as a team and get to know each other better."

The interns nodded excitedly, eager to get started. Victor handed each team their first clue and sent them off to explore the office.

As they walked around, the interns began to talk to their colleagues and work on the challenges. Sameer's team had to find a document with a specific reference number in the finance department, which they found with the help of his colleagues. Druv's team had to take a photo with a specific plant in the office, and Aarvi's team had to find a hidden message in a marketing campaign poster.

Inaya's team had to solve a puzzle in the IT department, and they quickly realized that one of the colleagues on their team had a knack for solving puzzles. As they worked together, they laughed and joked. Inaya felt grateful for the opportunity to connect with her colleagues in a fun and engaging way.

As they worked together, the interns got to know their colleagues deeper. They discovered common interests, shared experiences, and even learned new skills from one another. By the end of the scavenger hunt, the interns had formed strong bonds with their colleagues and felt like they had been part of the company for years.

After completing all the challenges, the teams gathered in the lobby, where Victor congratulated them on their hard work.

"Well done, everyone! I'm impressed by how well you all worked together. This is a great example of how building relationships with your colleagues can lead to success in the workplace. Keep up the good work!" Victor said, smiling.

Victor called all four interns to his office after the event. Aarvi, Inaya, Druv, and Sammer were excited. Victor quickly got into the subject, "Today, I'd like to share some tips with you on how to build strong relationships with your colleagues in the corporate world. Sound good?"

Sameer, "Yes, please! I'm excited to learn more."

Druv, "Absolutely, Victor. I think building relationships is important in any workplace."

Aarvi, "I agree. Having a strong network of people you can rely on is always good."

Inaya, "I'm interested to hear your thoughts on this, Victor. What are your top tips for building strong relationships with colleagues?"

Victor, "Well, first and foremost, effective communication is key. When communicating with your colleagues, being clear, concise, and respectful is important. Take the time to listen actively to what they're saying and respond thoughtfully. Avoid misunderstandings by clarifying any confusion before it becomes a bigger issue. Be open to feedback and constructive criticism, which will help you grow and improve."

Sameer, "That's helpful, Victor. Can you give us an example of how to use effective communication in the workplace?"

Victor, "Sure thing. Let's say you're working on a project with your team, and one of your colleagues has decided without consulting the rest of the group. Instead of getting upset or frustrated, approach your colleague calmly and professionally. Start by expressing your concerns and asking for an explanation for their decision. Listen attentively to their response and try to understand their point of view. Once you have all the information, explain your perspective and suggest a solution that benefits everyone involved."

Inaya, "Yes, I can see how effective communication can prevent misunderstandings and strengthen relationships."

Druv, "I think it's also important to resolve conflicts professionally."

Victor, "Well, conflict is inevitable in any workplace, but addressing it promptly and professionally is important. When conflicts arise, it's important to separate your emotions from the situation and focus on finding a solution that benefits everyone involved. It's about being open to compromise and listening to the other person's point of view."

Aarvi, "That sounds easier said than done. What if we have completely different ideas about approaching a project?"

Victor, "Great question, Aarvi. Let's say you prefer a more systematic and step-by-step process, while your colleague is more inclined to take risks and try new approaches. This is where conflict resolution comes in. You should approach the situation with an open mind and a willingness to compromise. Have an honest and respectful conversation with your colleague about your differing approaches. Try to understand their perspective and share your own in a non-confrontational manner. Once you've identified the core issue, work together to find a solution that works for both of you."

Sameer, "That makes sense. So, it's not about one person winning and the other losing. It's about finding a solution that works for both parties."

Victor, "Exactly, Sameer. Conflict resolution is about finding a compromise that allows both parties to bring their strengths to the table and achieve a more well-rounded result. It's important to remember that conflicts can also be an opportunity to learn and grow as a team."

Inaya, "Thanks for explaining that, Victor. It's good to know how to handle conflicts professionally."

Victor, "Of course, Inaya. Remember, conflict is a natural part of any workplace, but how you deal with it can make all the difference in your relationships with colleagues. By mastering conflict resolution skills, you can build stronger relationships and achieve greater success in the corporate world."

Victor, "Hey Sameer, Druv, Aarvi, and Inaya, have you all heard about the importance of networking in the corporate world?"

Sameer, "Yeah, I've heard about it, but I'm not sure where to start."

Victor, "Well, attending company events is a great way to get started. You can engage in conversations and get to know your colleagues personally. Building relationships can lead to a more positive work environment and increased job satisfaction."

Druv, "That sounds great, but what if we're at a conference with hundreds of people we don't know?"

Victor, "It's easy to stick with your colleagues, but branching out and meeting new people can be a valuable experience. Strike up a conversation with someone you admire or who shares your interests. Be genuine and interested in what they have to say, and offer to exchange contact information so you can stay in touch."

Aarvi, "I see what you're saying, but what's the point of building a network?"

Victor, "Building a strong network can lead to new opportunities and professional growth. You never know where a new connection can take you. For example, you might receive an email from someone you met who has a job opportunity that's perfect for you. Or, you might be able to collaborate on a project with someone you met who has complementary skills."

Inaya, "That makes sense. But how do we ensure we're not just using people for our benefit?"

Victor, "That's a great question. Networking is not just about what you can get from others but also about what you can offer. Be open to helping others with their projects or offering your skills and expertise. By building genuine relationships and being a valuable member of your professional community, you can build a network that will benefit you throughout your career."

Sameer, "Thanks for the advice, Victor. I'm going to start networking more intentionally now."

Druv, "Same here. It sounds like a great way to grow professionally."

Victor smiled at the interns, "Building strong relationships with your colleagues is crucial to success in the corporate world. Effective communication, conflict resolution, and networking are all important skills to master to build these relationships. Investing time and effort into building relationships with your colleagues will improve your work experience and increase your chances of achieving your career goals. Remember, success is not just about what you know, but also who you know."

As the interns finish meeting with Victor, they all thank him for his valuable advice and insights on building strong relationships with colleagues in the corporate world. Sameer, Druv, Aarvi, and Inaya are all motivated and inspired to put these tips into practice and start networking with their colleagues.

"Thank you so much, Victor," Sameer says as he leaves. "I appreciate you taking the time to meet with us and share your knowledge."

Druv nods in agreement. "Yes, thank you. I feel much more confident about building relationships with my colleagues now."

Aarvi says, "And I'm excited to start attending more company events and meeting new people."

Inaya smiles and adds, "I think it's great that we're all on the same page. Let's make an effort to support each other as we work on building our networks."

Victor nods in approval. "I'm glad to see that you all are taking this seriously. Building relationships takes time and effort but is worth it in the long run.
I'm looking forward to seeing your progress."

The interns say their goodbyes and head out of the office. As they walk to their cars, they discuss their plans for putting Victor's advice into action. They all feel excited and motivated to take their careers to the next level by building strong relationships with their colleagues.

Career growth and development

Aarvi, Druv, Sameer, and Inaya woke up early on Saturday, excited for casual dress day at their workplace. They all remembered the advice of their beloved CEO, Victor, on corporate dressing and dressed appropriately before heading to the office. They all were supposed to report to Victor's office in the morning.

They noticed four senior team members chit-chatting outside as they walked into his office on the 12th floor. They greeted them politely and walked towards Victor's office.
"Good morning, everyone," Victor greeted them warmly as they entered his office. "I have some exciting news to share with you all."

They all sat at the conference table adjacent to his office, eager to hear what Victor said.

"I am pleased to announce that we will be launching a 'Mentor Shadowing' program for our interns," Victor said, smiling.

The group looked at each other excitedly, wondering what the program would entail.

"This program will pair each of you with a mentor from our senior team, who will guide you for 2 weeks during your internship and provide valuable insights," Victor explained.

Aarvi's face lit up with enthusiasm. "Wow, that sounds amazing! Thank you so much, sir."

Druv nodded in agreement, "Yes, this is a fantastic opportunity. We're looking forward to it."

Inaya smiled, "Thank you so much, sir. We're grateful for this opportunity."

Victor looked pleased with their responses. "I have high hopes for all of you. This program will help you to develop your skills and gain experience in the industry."

Aarvi, who is interested in marketing, is paired with a senior marketing manager, Emma Herbert. During the shadowing program, Aarvi gets to observe Emma's day-to-day work activities, such as developing marketing campaigns, analyzing customer data, and managing a team of marketers.

Aarvi was thrilled as Emma had a wealth of experience in the industry, and Aarvi couldn't wait to learn from her.

During one of their shadowing sessions, Emma began to talk to Aarvi about setting career goals. "So, Aarvi, have you given much thought to your career goals?" Emma asked. Aarvi hesitated momentarily before responding, "I know that I'm interested in marketing, but beyond that, I'm not sure what my long-term career goals are."

Emma nodded understandingly. "That's okay. Setting clear and achievable goals is the first step toward career growth and development. Take some time to reflect on what you want to accomplish in your career."

She continued, "Start by setting both short-term and long-term goals. Short-term goals should be achievable within a year or less, while long-term goals may take several years. Be specific and write your goals down, as this helps to make them more tangible and achievable."

Aarvi listened intently, taking mental notes as Emma spoke. Emma then moved on to the topic of professional development opportunities.

"To reach your career goals, it's important to continuously improve your skills and knowledge," Emma said. "Seek out professional development opportunities, such as attending conferences, workshops, and training programs. These opportunities help you learn new skills and provide networking opportunities and a chance to connect with like-minded professionals in your field."

Aarvi nodded, "That makes a lot of sense. Thank you for sharing these insights with me, Emma."

Emma smiled, "You're welcome, Aarvi. Remember, setting clear goals and continuously learning and developing your skills is key to achieving success in your career."

Through the program, Aarvi gains a deeper understanding of the skills and knowledge required for a successful career in marketing and develops a mentorship relationship with Emma, who provides guidance and support for Aarvi's career development.

Druv, interested in finance, is paired with a mentor, Roy Baker, who has experience in various financial roles, such as investment banking, corporate finance, and accounting. Druv gets to shadow Rohit in each role, learning about the responsibilities and skills required for each.

During their Mentor Shadowing sessions, Druv had the opportunity to shadow Roy in each role, learning about the different responsibilities and skills required for each.

One day, Roy began to talk to Druv about building a network of supportive colleagues.

"Networking is crucial in our industry, Druv," Roy said. "A strong network of supportive colleagues can be invaluable in your career growth and development. Build relationships with others in your field, both inside and outside your organization. Attend industry events and join professional organizations to expand your network and make connections."

Druv nodded, taking in the advice. "That makes sense. It's important to have people you can rely on and learn from."
Roy then moved on to pursue further education or training programs.

"In some cases, pursuing further education or training programs may be necessary to achieve your career goals," Roy said. "Consider pursuing a degree, certification, or specialized training in your area of interest to gain the knowledge and skills necessary to succeed."

Druv thought for a moment before responding. "I've been considering pursuing a certification in financial planning. Do you think that would be a good idea?"

Roy smiled. "Absolutely. It's always a good idea to continue learning and developing your skills. Pursuing a certification or specialized training can set you apart from others and open up new opportunities."

Druv felt inspired by Roy's advice and was grateful for the opportunity to learn from him. "Thank you for sharing your insights with me, Roy," he said.

Roy smiled. "You're welcome, Druv. Always continue building your network and pursuing education and training opportunities to achieve your career goals."

Through the shadowing program, Druv gains a broader perspective on the finance function and develops a mentorship relationship with Rohit, who provides guidance and support for his career exploration.

Inaya, interested in human resources, pairs up with a senior HR manager, Kate. Inaya observes Kate's day-to-day work activities, such as recruitment, employee training and development, and performance management.

Inaya was excited to start her mentor shadowing program with senior HR manager Kate. As she followed Kate through her day-to-day work activities, Inaya observed how Kate managed employee training and development, recruitment, and performance management.

Kate turned to Inaya and said, "For career growth, it's important to understand your strengths and weaknesses." Inaya nodded, "Yes, I agree. I have been trying to identify my strengths and weaknesses, but it's difficult."

Kate smiled, "It can be difficult, but it's important to take the time to reflect on your skills and areas where you need improvement. Once you have identified your strengths and weaknesses, you can focus on building on your strengths and addressing your weaknesses."

Inaya replied, "That makes sense. How do you suggest I go about identifying my strengths and weaknesses?" Kate responded, "There are a few different methods. You can ask for feedback from colleagues and superiors, take assessments or personality tests, or reflect on your experiences and accomplishments. Once you have identified your strengths, you can focus on building them up even further. And for your weaknesses, you can work on developing those areas through training or mentorship."

Inaya smiled, "Thank you for the advice, Kate. I will keep that in mind as I continue to grow in my career."

Kate replied, "You're welcome, Inaya. Another important tool for career growth is mentorship and coaching. Find someone with experience in your interest, and ask them to be your mentor. A good mentor can guide, advise, and support you as you work towards your career goals."

Through the shadowing program, Inaya gains valuable insights into the skills and knowledge required for a successful HR career and develops a mentorship relationship with Kate, who provides guidance and support for Inaya's career growth.

Finally, Sameer, interested in technology, is paired with a mentor, Simon Morgan, who has experience in various technology roles, such as software engineering, product management, and data analysis. Sameer gets to shadow Raj in these roles, learning about the responsibilities and skills required for each.

On his first day of the mentor shadowing program, Sameer was excited to meet his mentor, Simon Morgan. As he entered Simon's office, he was greeted with a warm smile and a firm handshake.

Simon began, "So, Sameer, I'm excited to have you shadow me and learn about the different roles in technology. Today we'll start with software engineering, but before we dive into that, I want to talk to you about developing leadership skills."

Sameer was intrigued and leaned in closer. "What do you mean by leadership skills, Simon?"

"Well, Sameer," Simon began, "If you aspire to leadership roles in your career, developing the skills necessary to be an effective leader is important. This includes developing communication skills, delegating effectively, and cultivating emotional intelligence."

Sameer nodded, "I see. And how can I develop these skills?"

Simon replied, "One way to develop these skills is through hands-on experience. Take on leadership roles in your projects or volunteer for leadership positions in clubs or organizations. You can also attend workshops or training sessions on leadership development."

Sameer took notes as Simon continued, "Another important aspect of career growth is regularly assessing your progress. Set regular checkpoints to measure progress towards your goals, and make adjustments as necessary. Celebrate your successes along the way. Don't be afraid to ask for feedback from colleagues and mentors to help you continue to grow and develop."

Sameer thanked Simon for the valuable advice and looked forward to shadowing him in the software engineering role later that day.

Through a week, Sameer gains a broader perspective on the technology industry. Also, he develops a mentorship relationship with Raj, who provides guidance and support for his career exploration.

It was Victor's turn to take feedback after a weeklong "Mentor Shadowing" program.

Victor called Aarvi, Druv, Sameer, and Inaya to his office. They arrived one by one, and Victor welcomed them warmly.

"Welcome, everyone," Victor said as they settled into their seats. "I hope you've all had a chance to reflect on your experiences during the Mentor Shadowing program."

"Yes, it was a great experience for me," Aarvi said, nodding in agreement. "I learned a lot about marketing strategies and team management from my mentor, Emma."

"I agree," Sameer added. "My mentor, Simon, was great. I learned about software engineering, product management, and data analysis. It was a valuable experience."

Druv and Inaya nodded in agreement, and Victor smiled. "I'm glad to hear that," he said. "Did anyone have any specific takeaways or lessons learned from the program?"

"I learned that setting clear career goals is important," Inaya said. "Knowing what you want to achieve and how you plan to get there is important."
"I also learned the importance of building a strong network," Druv added. "Having supportive colleagues and mentors can make all the difference in your career growth."

"Those are great takeaways," Victor said, nodding. "Anything else?"

"I learned that developing leadership skills is important if you want to grow in your career," Sameer said. "And it's important to regularly assess your progress and make adjustments along the way."
Victor smiled. "Those are all excellent points," he said. "I'm glad you all had a positive experience with the program. We'll keep this in mind for future professional development opportunities."

The group continued to chat about their experiences over coffee, exchanging ideas and insights on their respective fields. It was clear that the Mentor Shadowing program had been a valuable experience for all of them.

As Aarvi, Inaya, Druv, and Sameer left Victor's office, they couldn't help but feel a sense of satisfaction after their feedback session.

"Wow, that was productive," said Sameer.

"I agree," said Inaya. "It was great to hear everyone's experiences and learnings from the shadowing program."
"And getting concrete advice on developing our careers was helpful," added Aarvi.

Aarvi, Inaya, Druv, and Sameer walked out of Victor's office building, feeling satisfied after their feedback session with him. They chatted excitedly about what they had learned from their mentors and how they planned to apply it to their careers.

As they reached the main door of the building, they turned around to see Victor watching them from his 12th-floor office window. They waved goodbye to him, and he smiled back at them with pride. The four of them walked away, grateful for the opportunity to participate in the mentor shadowing program and excited for the future.

Navigating office politics

Aarvi, Inaya, Druv, and Sameer were bright-eyed and bushy-tailed as they interned at the famous tech company led by the renowned CEO, Victor Edmund. They were excited to use their knowledge and skills in the real world, learn from the best in the business, and gain valuable experience that would help them shape their careers.

The four interns were highly dedicated to their work and would arrive at the office early to make the most of their time there. They would settle down at their workstations, pull out their laptops, and start working on their assigned tasks with utmost precision and attention to detail. They were determined to deliver their best performance and make a lasting impression on their superiors. They would also take the initiative to ask questions, seek feedback, and improve their work to the best of their ability.

Despite their busy schedule, the interns would always find time to bond with each other over a quick coffee break or lunch. They would exchange stories about their day's work and new colleagues.

As the day ended, the interns would pack up their work and head out for leisure activities in the city. They would explore the sights and sounds of London, try out new restaurants and cuisines, and make memories that would last a lifetime.

Overall, Aarvi, Inaya, Druv, and Sameer were well on their way to becoming true professionals. They were determined to make the most of their internship experience.

However, their initial excitement was short-lived. After just a few days of working at the company, the interns realized that office politics was a harsh reality they had not anticipated. They witnessed firsthand how colleagues would engage in subtle and not-so-subtle maneuvers to further their interests, often at the expense of others and even the company itself.

In this environment, it was not uncommon for colleagues to take credit for other people's work, undermine each other's efforts, spread rumors and gossip, or engage in other manipulative tactics. The interns saw how some employees would engage in power plays, favoritism, and cliques to gain an edge, even if it meant compromising the company's success.

For instance, Aarvi was thrilled to be assigned to work on a project with a colleague known for being highly skilled and experienced in their field. She hoped to learn from this colleague and collaborate to produce an outstanding result for the company. However, it wasn't long before she began to feel uneasy. The colleague seemed more interested in taking credit for their work than working together to produce a successful outcome. Aarvi felt frustrated and undervalued and wondered how she would ever be able to make an impact in such a cut-throat environment.

Similarly, Inaya heard gossip about a senior executive rumored to have been involved romantically with his junior. She shared this information with a trusted colleague, hoping to gain insight into the situation and perhaps even offer assistance. However, the information quickly spread throughout the office, and Inaya was the target of scrutiny and suspicion. She felt betrayed by her colleague and was concerned about the potential impact on her prospects at the company.

The interns realized they had much to learn about navigating this complex and often treacherous environment. They knew that they needed to find ways to establish themselves as valuable contributors to the company while also avoiding getting caught up in the politics that seemed to dominate the workplace.

During a team meeting, Victor Edmund noticed the interns' discomfort and frustration one day. He addressed the issue head-on and shared his experiences with office politics. He explained that competition and conflicting interests were natural in any workplace. Still, it was essential to maintain a positive attitude and focus on the bigger picture.

Victor, the CEO of a large tech company, sat down with a group of interns, Aarvi, Inaya, Druv, and Sameer, to discuss the topic of office politics.

"Alright, guys, today we'll talk about office politics. It's a crucial aspect of the corporate world that can make or break your success in the workplace," Victor began.

The interns listened as Victor continued, "In any workplace, some individuals hold more power and influence than others. It's important to understand the dynamics at play and identify who holds the most sway and influence."

Druv raised his hand and asked, "But how do we do that? How do we figure out who has the most power?"

Victor smiled, "Great question, Druv. It's all about observation. Pay attention to how decisions are made and who is involved in those decision-making processes. Take note of who holds regular meetings with other higher-ups and who seems to have a lot of influence over their colleagues."

Inaya said, "Okay, so we understand the power structure, but how do we communicate effectively in this environment?"

Victor nodded, "Another great question, Inaya. Effective communication is key. It's important to be clear and concise in your communication and respectful of differing opinions and perspectives. If you're working on a project with someone who tends to dominate conversations, like Sarah, try speaking up and asserting your ideas while also actively listening to the ideas of others."

Sameer looked uncertain and asked, "But what if we have a manager with a different communication style than us?"

Victor replied, "It's important to adapt your communication style to better align with your manager's preferences while communicating your ideas effectively. This shows that you can work well with others and be flexible."

Aarvi spoke up, "But what about office gossip and drama? How do we avoid getting caught up in that?"

Victor nodded solemnly, "That's a common pitfall you must avoid. Getting caught up in office gossip or drama can quickly erode your reputation and make building positive relationships with your colleagues difficult. Focus on building positive relationships instead of engaging in negative talk."

The interns listened carefully and took notes as Victor explained the ins and outs of navigating office politics. By the end of the conversation, they felt more confident and equipped to handle the challenges of the corporate world.

"Office politics can be tricky, but with the right strategies, you can navigate it like a pro. First things first, you need to avoid common pitfalls that can negatively impact your reputation and relationships within the workplace," Victor continued.

Aarvi raised her hand. "What kind of pitfalls, Victor?"

"Well, for example, getting caught up in office gossip or drama. Trust me, it's tempting to join in and vent your frustrations, but it's not worth it. Instead, focus on building positive relationships with your colleagues and contribute positively to the team," Victor explained.

Inaya nodded in agreement. "That makes sense. What about taking sides or aligning too closely with one particular individual or group?"

"Exactly. Avoid that at all costs. Maintain positive relationships with everyone, even if they have differing opinions or ways of doing things," Victor said.

Druv said, "So, how do we maintain those positive relationships?"

"By remaining professional and respectful in all your interactions with colleagues and superiors. Avoid negative or confrontational language, and instead focus on constructive and positive communication," Victor replied.

Sameer leaned forward. "Thanks, Victor. This is constructive advice."
"No problem, Sameer. Just remember, understanding office politics is key to success in any workplace. Good luck out there," Victor said with a smile.

Victor concludes his talk on office politics with a smile, "Remember, navigating office politics can be a challenge, but with the right approach, you can succeed. It's all about finding the right balance between assertiveness and diplomacy. Don't be afraid to speak up and share your ideas, but also be willing to listen to others and work collaboratively. And always remember to be professional and respectful and avoid common pitfalls like office gossip and taking sides. With these strategies in mind, I do not doubt that you all will excel in your careers and build strong relationships within the workplace."

Aarvi, Inaya, Druv, and Sameer nod in agreement, feeling empowered and ready to tackle the challenges of office politics. "Thank you, Victor," they say in unison. "We'll keep these strategies in mind and work hard to build positive relationships with our colleagues and superiors."

As Aarvi, Inaya, Druv, and Sameer walked out of Victor's office, they couldn't help but feel relieved and more confident in navigating office politics.

"I'm so glad we had that talk with Victor," Inaya said. "I was feeling so lost about handling the office dynamics, but now I feel like I have some strategies to use."

Druv nodded in agreement. "Yes, learning about the power structure and how to communicate effectively with colleagues and superiors was helpful. I think I will start paying closer attention to the decision-making processes and who holds the most influence in the company."

Aarvi said, "And it's important to avoid getting caught up in office gossip or drama. It's easy to get sucked in, but it can harm your reputation and relationships with your colleagues."

Sameer nodded. "And we can't forget about the importance of diplomacy. We need to be confident in our ideas and willing to compromise and work collaboratively with others."

As they reached their workspace, the interns felt more equipped to navigate the political landscape of the office. They were excited to put their newfound knowledge and strategies into practice and build positive relationships with their colleagues and superiors.

Balancing work and personal life

Dayita Joseph arrived in London for the Annual HR Conference, where she would be one of the keynote speakers. She had been looking forward to this conference for months. She was excited to share her knowledge and expertise with fellow HR professionals worldwide.

After her session at the conference, Dayita received a message from Victor. They had met at a previous conference and developed a close relationship. Victor wanted to catch up with Dayita.

Dayita was thrilled to hear from Victor and agreed to meet him after the conference. They decided to meet at Victor's office in the heart of London. Upon entering the premises, she was greeted by the receptionist, who informed her that the CEO, Victor, was waiting for her. She was pleasantly surprised and quickly walked onto the elevator to Victor's office.

As Dayita walked into his office on the 12th floor, she was greeted by Victor's warm smile. They hugged and exchanged pleasantries before settling down at a table.

As they chatted in his office, Victor mentioned that Aarvi, Inaya, Druv, and Sameer from Bengaluru were interning at his firm in London.

Victor and Dayita decided to drop in and see how the interns were getting along. When they arrived, they found Aarvi, Inaya, Druv, and Sameer sitting in a conference room, discussing their work.

Dayita started the conversation by asking the interns about their experience working in London. "So, how's everything going with your internships?" she asked.

Aarvi replied, "It's been great, but the workload can sometimes be overwhelming."

Victor nodded and said, "That's understandable, but finding a balance between work and personal life is important. Dayita, what do you think?"

Dayita smiled and said, "I completely agree, Victor. The first step to finding balance is setting boundaries. Establishing clear boundaries between work and personal life is crucial, both physically and mentally. For example, leaving work at the office and not checking emails after hours."

Victor agreed, "Establishing clear boundaries between work and personal life is crucial."

Dayita continued, "It's easy to get caught up in work and allow it to bleed over into your personal life, but building physical and mental boundaries can help you disengage and prioritize your personal life."

Inaya asked, "But how do you establish these boundaries?" Druv added, "Especially when your job requires you to always be available."

Victor nodded, "It can be challenging, but it's essential to consciously separate work and personal life. For example, you can create physical boundaries by leaving work at the office, not checking emails after hours, and not bringing work home."

Dayita continued, "It's also important to prioritize your personal life by setting aside time for self-care activities like exercise, meditation, or spending time with loved ones."

Sameer asked, "But what about stress? How do you manage that?"

Victor replied, "Stress management is also crucial to finding balance. Techniques like deep breathing, mindfulness, and time management can help reduce stress and promote a healthier work-life balance."

Aarvi added, "I can relate to that. In my previous job, I found it hard to disconnect from work, affecting my personal life. But after setting boundaries, I feel more relaxed and focused during work hours and enjoy my personal life."

Dayita smiled, "That's great to hear, Aarvi. Establishing boundaries can be challenging, but it's a necessary step towards maintaining overall well-being and finding balance in life."

Victor and Dayita continued their conversation on balancing work and personal life by discussing the importance of self-care.

Dayita said, "Self-care is essential to maintain a healthy work-life balance. We often prioritize work over ourselves, but neglecting self-care can lead to burnout and decreased job satisfaction."

Victor said, "As interns, you are all ambitious and driven individuals, but it's important to remember that your well-being is just as important as your professional growth. Neglecting self-care can lead to burnout and decreased job satisfaction, which is not good for you or the company."

Dayita added, "That's right. We understand that work demands can be high, but taking care of yourself should always be a priority. Let me give you an example. Nikita, a software developer, spent long hours sitting in front of her computer, which caused back pain and muscle tension. She decided to take breaks throughout the day to stretch and walk around. In addition, she committed to exercising regularly, whether going for a run or attending a yoga class. This helped her manage her stress levels and improve her physical health, increasing her energy and productivity at work."

Aarvi, one of the interns, said, "I agree, but sometimes it can be hard to find the time for self-care when work is demanding. How do we balance our work and personal life?"

Druv, another intern, added, "Yes, and sometimes, it feels like we have to choose between work and our personal life."

Victor nodded and said, "It's a common struggle, but finding a balance is important. For example, Sam, a marketing specialist, found that he was spending too much time at work and not enough time with his loved ones. He consciously tried to schedule regular outings with his friends and family, such as going to a movie or having a game night. This helped him recharge and reconnect with his loved ones, increasing happiness and reducing stress levels."

Dayita chimed in, "Exactly. Balancing work and personal life requires planning and prioritization. You need to schedule your time effectively and ensure that you're taking care of yourself and fulfilling your professional responsibilities."

Inaya added, "It's important to communicate with your supervisor if you need some time off to take care of yourself or to attend to a personal matter. Most organizations understand their employees' need for self-care and personal time."

Victor concluded the topic by saying, "In summary, prioritizing self-care is essential for maintaining a healthy work-life balance. It's not about choosing between work and personal life but finding a balance that allows you to thrive in both areas. We hope you will take these lessons seriously and implement them in your personal and professional lives."

"Managing stress is crucial to maintaining a healthy work-life balance," Dayita said. "Stress can impact your productivity and overall well-being. One effective way to manage stress is through deep breathing exercises."

Inaya spoke up. "I've been doing that lately, and it's helped me stay focused and less stressed."

"Exactly," Dayita said. "Taking a few minutes to practice deep breathing exercises can help you reset and refocus your mind."

Druv, another intern, added, "I also find mindfulness helpful for managing stress. It helps me stay present and focused on the task at hand."

"Yes, mindfulness is another great technique for managing stress," Victor said. "It involves being present at the moment and focusing on one's thoughts and feelings without judgment."

Sameer spoke up. "Effective time management is key to managing stress and achieving a healthy work-life balance." Victor nodded. "That's true, Sameer. Prioritizing tasks, setting realistic deadlines, and avoiding over-commitment can help reduce stress levels and increase productivity."

"I use a task management app to prioritize my work tasks and set achievable deadlines," Sameer said. "It helps me avoid feeling overwhelmed and ensures that I can manage my workload effectively, leading to a more balanced life."

"Great job, everyone," Dayita said. "Managing stress is crucial to maintaining a healthy work-life balance, and these techniques can help you achieve that. Remember to take care of yourselves and make time for self-care."

Victor and Dayita looked at the interns with a sense of pride. They had just spent the afternoon coaching them on balancing work and personal life. They felt that they had imparted some valuable knowledge.

"So, what have you learned today?" Victor asked.

Aarvi raised her hand eagerly. "I learned that setting boundaries is important. I always used to feel guilty about saying no to work tasks. Still, I know it's okay to prioritize my personal life sometimes."

Inaya nodded in agreement. "And I learned that caring for my physical and mental health is crucial. I will start incorporating more exercise and deep breathing into my daily routine."

Druv chimed in. "I found the mindfulness techniques helpful. Getting caught up in work stress is so easy, but taking a few minutes to clear my mind has been beneficial."

Sameer added, "And I learned that effective time management is key. By prioritizing my tasks and setting achievable goals, I can avoid feeling overwhelmed and achieve a more balanced life."

Victor smiled. "Exactly. You can achieve a healthy work-life balance by setting boundaries, prioritizing self-care, and managing stress levels. And remember, taking care of yourself is beneficial for your health and can lead to increased productivity and success in the workplace."

Dayita nodded. "That's right. Remembering that work is just one aspect of our lives is important. We must make time for our personal lives and care for ourselves to achieve overall well-being."

The interns thanked Victor and Dayita for their valuable coaching. They left the room feeling inspired and empowered to implement these techniques daily.

As the interns left, Victor and Dayita couldn't help but feel a sense of relief. The day had been long and exhausting, but they had survived. Finally, it was time for them to relax.

Victor turned to Dayita and asked, "Would you like to catch up later? Maybe we could go to our favorite restaurant in London?"

Dayita smiled, "That sounds like a great idea! I could use a good meal and some company."

They agreed to meet up at the restaurant later in the evening. Victor went home to freshen up and change while Dayita finished some work from her hotel.

Finally, it was time for their dinner date. Dayita arrived at the restaurant, and Victor was already waiting for her. The restaurant was in a posh location in London, and the ambiance was cozy and inviting.

As they sat down, they perused the menu and placed their orders. While waiting for their food, they began to catch up on their professional and personal lives. They talked about their passions, dreams, and aspirations and found that they had a lot in common. Victor admired Dayita's drive and determination, and Dayita was impressed by Victor's ability to navigate the corporate world with ease.

As they enjoyed their delicious meals, they continued to chat and laugh. They bonded over their love of music, and Victor even shared his hidden talent for playing the guitar.

The evening flew by quickly; before they knew it, it was time to leave. They exchanged hugs and promised to stay in touch. Victor walked Dayita to her car, and they said their goodbyes.

As Dayita drove to her hotel, she couldn't help but feel grateful for the beautiful evening. Victor, too, felt a sense of contentment as he drove back home. He had enjoyed spending time with Dayita and looked forward to possibly developing this relationship further.

It was a reminder that even in a fast-paced world, enjoying good company and delicious food can do wonders for the soul.

Staying up to date with industry trends

In the bustling city of London, Aarvi, Druv, Inaya, and Sameer were four young students who had recently joined a Tech company for their internship. They were thrilled to be a part of such a dynamic and innovative industry, and they dove headfirst into their work.

At first, everything was going great, and they felt they were on top of the world. But then, they realized that the tech industry was a fast-paced and ever-changing world. They started to feel like they were falling behind and were missing out on great opportunities.

Sameer, while working on a project, ran into a complex problem. They had been using what they thought was the best software tool in the market, but they soon realized that a new and better tool had been released. Sameer was stunned that they had not heard about it earlier and felt they had missed out on a great opportunity.

At the same time, Aarvi was working on a new campaign and was targeting her audience using traditional marketing methods. However, she soon discovered that her target audience was most active on social media. She realized she had missed out on a significant opportunity by not keeping up with the latest marketing trends.

But Aarvi, Druv, Inaya, and Sameer were not the kind of people to sit back and let opportunities pass them by. They knew they had to stay updated with the latest trends and tools in their industry. So, they set out to learn as much as they could.

Sameer decided to speak up about the issue. He went to the HR department and explained his concerns to them. The HR Head listened carefully and understood Sameer's problem. The HR Head realized that the issue was not limited to Sameer alone and that Aarvi, Druv, and Inaya might face similar problems.

The HR Head met with all four interns to discuss their concerns. During the meeting, the interns expressed concerns about falling behind in the industry and not knowing about the latest tools and trends. The HR Head understood their concerns and advised them to attend a Tech conference in London next week. The HR Head explained that the conference would be an excellent opportunity for them to learn about the latest industry trends and innovations and to network with other professionals in the field.

Aarvi, Druv, Inaya, and Sameer were thrilled to attend the upcoming Tech conference in London. But before they could finalize their plans, they knew they had to get approval from the CEO, Victor. They scheduled a meeting with him, hoping to convince him of the importance of attending the conference.

As they entered Victor's office, they noticed how impressive it looked with its floor-to-ceiling windows and sleek furniture. But their nerves quickly kicked in as they saw Victor sitting behind his large wooden desk, staring at them with piercing eyes.

"Good afternoon, Victor," Aarvi said, trying to hide her nervousness.

"Good afternoon, Aarvi, Druv, Inaya, and Sameer," Victor replied, gesturing for them to sit. "What brings you here today?"

"We wanted to talk to you about the Tech conference in London next week," Sameer said confidently.

"The HR Head suggested that we attend the conference to stay up to date with industry trends," Inaya added, looking at Victor for approval.

Victor leaned back in his chair, his eyes glancing at each in turn. "Hmm, interesting," he said, rubbing his chin thoughtfully. "And what do you hope to gain from this conference?"

"We hope to acquire new skills and learn about the latest advancements in the tech industry," Druv replied.
"We need to stay ahead of the competition, Victor," Aarvi added, trying to sound as convincing as possible.

Victor listened intently, nodding his head in agreement. "I see your point," he said. "The tech industry is constantly evolving, and staying current with the latest trends and technologies is important."

The interns exchanged excited glances, happy that Victor understood the importance of the conference.

Victor wanted to ensure that the interns understood the importance of staying up to date with industry trends, so he took a seat and began to speak with them in a conversational tone.

"Alright, guys, let me tell you why staying updated with industry trends is so important," he began. "In any field, it's crucial to remain relevant and competitive. Whether you're an entrepreneur or a seasoned executive, you need to know what's happening in your industry."

The interns nodded, looking interested in what Victor had to say.
"By staying updated with industry trends, you can identify new opportunities and potential challenges," Victor continued. "This will help you adapt your strategies and maintain a competitive advantage over your peers."

"That makes sense," said Aarvi. "But can you give us an example?"

"Sure, let's take the tech industry," said Victor. "There has been a significant shift towards developing artificial intelligence and machine learning technologies in recent years. By staying current with these trends, businesses can identify potential applications for these technologies and develop strategies to integrate them into their operations."

"I see," said Druv, nodding in agreement. "So, by staying up to date, we can be proactive and find ways to improve our company's performance."

"Exactly!" said Victor. "Now, let's consider the healthcare industry. Medical technology advancements have revolutionized how healthcare professionals diagnose and treat illnesses. By staying current with these trends, medical professionals can improve patient outcomes, reduce costs, and stay ahead of the curve."

Inaya spoke up. "That's a great example. Staying current with industry trends can give us a significant competitive advantage."

Victor smiled. "I'm glad you guys understand. Attending the Tech conference in London is a great opportunity for you to learn about the latest advancements in the industry and acquire new skills. I encourage you to make the most of it."
Victor continued discussing with the interns and elaborated on the importance of attending industry events. "As I mentioned earlier, attending industry events like CES is an excellent way to stay up to date with the latest trends and developments," he said. The interns nodded in agreement, showing their interest in learning more. Victor continued, "At these events, you hear from industry experts and thought leaders, which can be incredibly valuable. You also network with peers and potential partners, which can lead to new business opportunities and partnerships."

Inaya, who was particularly interested in attending industry events, asked, "But how do we know which events to attend?"

Victor smiled and replied, "That's a great question, Inaya. There are several ways to find out about industry events. One way is to check industry publications, such as trade magazines and websites, which often feature upcoming events. Another way is to ask if any colleagues or peers are attending events you might be interested in. And finally, you can search online for events related to your industry and location."

Druv, intrigued by the idea of attending CES, asked, "What can we expect to gain from attending an event like CES?"

Victor replied, "CES is one of the world's largest and most important technology events. You can expect to see the latest technology products and innovations at this event, hear from industry experts and thought leaders, and network with peers and potential partners. It's a unique opportunity to gain insights into the future of technology and build relationships with other professionals in the industry."

Victor took a sip of his coffee and turned to the interns. "Now, let's talk about industry publications," he said. "They're a fantastic way to stay updated with your field's latest trends and developments. Do any of you currently read any industry publications?"

Aarvi raised her hand. "I follow a few tech blogs online," she said. "They usually post about new products and emerging trends in the industry."

"That's great, Aarvi," Victor said. "Reading online publications is a convenient way to stay informed. But it's also important to read traditional print publications as well. They can provide in-depth analysis and insights you might not find online."

Inaya nodded in agreement. "I subscribe to a few fashion magazines, and they always have interesting articles about emerging designers and fashion trends," she said.

"Exactly," Victor said. "Reading industry publications is a tried and tested way to stay updated with your field's latest trends and developments. They can provide insights into emerging trends, market conditions, and industry events. And, as Inaya mentioned, they're a great way to learn about emerging designers and other businesses in your field."
Druv spoke up. "What if I don't have time to read industry publications regularly?" he asked.

Victor smiled. "That's a great question, Druv. Many publications now have online versions that can be accessed easily and conveniently anywhere. You can also sign up for newsletters or alerts, which can summarize the latest news and developments in your field. That way, you can stay informed even if you're on the go or working remotely."

"Alright, Now let's talk about networking and staying up to date with industry trends," he said, leaning forward in his chair. "This is a crucial aspect of professional development that can help you stay ahead of the curve in your field."

The interns nodded in agreement, eager to learn more.

"One way to stay current is by attending events and conferences in your industry," Victor explained. "For example, if you're interested in marketing, attending events like Marketing Week Live or Content Marketing World can be incredibly beneficial. You'll get to hear from experts in the field and network with other professionals."

Inaya perked up. "What if we can't attend in-person events?" she asked.

Victor replied. "In that case, you can join professional associations like the American Marketing Association or the Chartered Institute of Marketing. They offer many resources, including industry publications, webinars, and networking events you can attend virtually."

Druv chimed in. "What about online forums and groups? Are those useful too?"

"Definitely," Victor said with a smile. "Participating in online forums and groups, such as LinkedIn groups or Reddit threads, can be a great way to connect with other professionals in your field, ask questions, and share insights and ideas. Just be sure to engage respectfully and professionally."

Aarvi nodded. "That all makes sense. So, attending events, joining professional associations, and participating in online groups can all help us stay updated with industry trends?"

"Exactly," Victor said, nodding. "By doing these things, you can stay informed, connect with other professionals, and make informed business decisions. It's all about staying ahead of the curve and being proactive in professional development."

"Well, that's it for today, folks! I hope you found this discussion helpful in understanding the importance of staying up to date with industry trends," said Victor, the CEO of the tech company, as he wrapped up his mentorship session with interns Aarvi, Inaya, Druv, and Sameer.

"It's been informative," said Aarvi. "I didn't realize how important it was to attend events and join professional associations."

"Absolutely," replied Victor. "Attending events and joining professional associations can provide valuable opportunities to meet like-minded professionals and stay up to date with the latest industry trends."

"I also found it interesting how reading industry publications can help us stay informed about the latest economic policies, business developments, and market trends," added Inaya.

"Exactly!" said Victor. "Industry publications such as The Economist or The Financial Times can provide valuable insights to help you make informed business decisions."

"And let's not forget about the importance of networking," said Druv. "I think joining online forums and groups can be a great way to connect with other professionals and learn from their experiences."

"Absolutely," agreed Victor. "Participating in online forums and groups can provide a platform for discussion and collaboration, helping you to stay up to date with the latest trends and developments in your industry."

"And at the end of the day, the most important thing is to be proactive and stay ahead of the curve," said Sameer. "Thanks, Victor, for such an informative session!"

"No problem, Sameer! It was my pleasure to share my insights with you all," said Victor. "Remember, the world is constantly changing, and keeping up with industry trends is essential to stay relevant and succeed in today's fast-paced world."

"Keep me updated on your experience," he said as they left his office. The interns felt relieved and grateful for the support of their CEO. They were now more motivated than ever to attend the conference and learn as much as possible. They went back to start preparing for the conference

Preparing for the future and setting career goals

It was the final day of the internship at the famous tech company in London, and Aarvi, Druv, Sameer, and Inaya were feeling a mix of emotions. They had come a long way since they started their internship in London. They worked on various projects, learned new skills, and made some great friends along the way. And now, as they walked towards the conference room for their final meeting with the CEO, Victor Edmund, they couldn't help but feel a mix of emotions.

Aarvi, who had always been shy, was now more confident and outspoken. Druv struggled with time management and had learned to prioritize his work and meet deadlines. Sameer had initially found it hard to work in a team and had become an excellent team player. And Inaya, unsure about her career path, had found her passion for data analytics.

As they entered the conference room, they were greeted by the sight of Victor sitting at the head of the table with a warm smile.

"Welcome, Aarvi, Druv, Sameer, and Inaya," he said. "I can't believe how fast these six months have gone by. You have all done an excellent job, and I'm proud of your progress."
They all smiled, feeling a sense of pride and accomplishment.
Victor continued, "Now, as you progress in your careers, I want to share some advice with you."

"Internships are a great way to learn and gain valuable experience," he said. "But it's also important to use this time to think about your long-term career goals and start planning for your future."

As Aarvi, Inaya, Druv, and Sameer sat down in the conference room for their final meeting with the CEO, Victor Edmund, they were nervous yet excited to hear what he had to say. Victor began by sharing his story of building his career in the tech industry through careful planning and perseverance.

"Preparing for the future is essential," he said, "especially in the tech industry, where things change rapidly. To succeed, you need to be adaptable, resilient, and always learning."
He explained the importance of setting both short-term and long-term goals. "Short-term goals help you stay motivated and feel like you're making progress, but long-term goals give you a sense of direction and purpose. They help you stay focused and ensure you're moving in the right direction."

Inaya spoke up, "But what if unexpected opportunities arise? How do we stay on track with our goals?"

Victor smiled, "Inaya. It's essential to have a flexible plan that can adapt to changing circumstances. You never know what opportunities might come your way, so it's essential to be open to them and adjust your goals as needed."

Druv asked, "Can you give us an example of someone who set long-term goals and achieved success?"

Victor nodded, "Absolutely. Let me tell you about Jennifer working in the IT Department. She always had a passion for technology but pursued a different field in college. After a few years of working in that field, she realized she wasn't happy and decided to change. Jennifer set herself a long-term goal of becoming a software engineer. She started taking online courses to learn the basics. She worked hard, networked with people in the industry, and eventually landed an entry-level job at a software company."

Victor continued, "Jennifer didn't stop there. She continued to set and achieve new goals, always keeping her long-term goal in mind. Over time, she was promoted to a more senior role and eventually landed a dream job at a major tech company. Jennifer's story shows us the power of setting long-term goals and working towards them with determination and flexibility."

Victor encouraged Aarvi, Inaya, Druv, and Sameer to start thinking about their long-term goals and developing a flexible plan. "Remember," he said, "success in the tech industry requires hard work, dedication, and a willingness to adapt. But anything is possible with the right mindset and a clear plan."

"As you all know," he began, "Industries are constantly evolving, and it's important to stay ahead of the curve to remain competitive. This entails investing in yourself and your talents to raise your value to your employer and your job market marketability."
Aarvi raised her hand. "But how do we know which skills to invest in?" she asked.

"Great question," Victor replied. "One way to identify areas for improvement is to look at your current job and the industry as a whole. Are there any high-demand skills or competencies that could help you excel in your current role? For example, learning about social media marketing or SEO could be valuable if you're interested in marketing. Or, if you work in technology, learning a new programming language or development tool could be beneficial."

Inaya nodded in agreement. "But what if we're unsure how to develop those skills?"

"That's where mentorship and coaching come in," Victor explained. "Finding a mentor or coach with experience in your desired area can be incredibly helpful. They can provide guidance, feedback, and support as you develop new competencies."

Druv chimed in. "But what if we don't have the time or resources to pursue formal education or take courses?"

Victor smiled. "Investing in yourself doesn't necessarily mean pursuing formal education or courses. It can also mean seeking opportunities to learn on the job or through industry events and conferences. It is important to continuously learn and improve, even if it's just a little bit at a time."

Sameer spoke up. "But how do we know if our investment in ourselves is paying off?"

Victor leaned forward. "It may not always be immediately clear, but you'll see the rewards of your hard work and dedication over time. Just like planting a seed that will grow and bear fruit in the future, investing in yourself and your skills will lead to greater opportunities, job satisfaction, and career fulfillment."

The interns listened as Victor shared his wisdom and experience.

"I also want to talk to you about the importance of adaptability in your career. In today's fast-paced world, it's important to be able to adapt to change and navigate uncertainty," said Victor

The interns listened as Victor shared the story of Jane, the financial analyst in his tech company who could adapt to a new job in a different field. He emphasized how her ability to adapt allowed her to thrive in her new role and make a meaningful impact in her organization.

"As you progress in your careers, you will undoubtedly face challenges and changes," Victor continued. "It's important to be open to new possibilities and willing to take on new challenges, even if they may be outside your comfort zone." Inaya said, "But how can we develop this adaptability, Victor?"

Victor replied. "One way to develop adaptability is to stay curious and keep learning. The more knowledge and skills you have, the better you will be to handle new challenges." Druv nodded in agreement, "That makes sense, Victor. What else can we do?"

"Another way to develop adaptability is to be open to feedback and constructive criticism," Victor said. "When you receive feedback, take it as an opportunity to learn and grow rather than a personal attack."

Sameer said, "But what if we don't know how to adapt to a specific situation?"

"In those cases, don't be afraid to ask for help or seek guidance from others," Victor replied. "You can always contact mentors, colleagues, or other professionals in your network for advice and support."

The interns listened intently, eager to learn more. Victor continued, "Setting goals can help you focus your efforts and stay motivated towards achieving your desired success. Setting SMART goals - specific, measurable, achievable, relevant, and time-bound - is important to ensure you have a clear plan to reach your objectives."

Aarvi raised her hand and asked, "But how do we know what goals to set for ourselves? I'm not sure where I want to be in five years."

Victor smiled, "That's a great question, Aarvi. Setting career goals starts with knowing yourself and understanding your strengths and passions. Take the time to reflect on what you enjoy doing, what skills you excel at, and what kind of impact you want to make in the world. From there, you can start setting goals that align with your values and aspirations."

Inaya chimed in, "But what if our goals change over time? How do we stay on track?"

Victor nodded, "That's a valid concern, Inaya. It's important to remember that goals can evolve as we grow and gain new experiences. The key is to stay flexible and adapt to new opportunities and challenges. Review your goals periodically and adjust if necessary to ensure they are still relevant and achievable."

Druv asked, "What about setbacks? How do we stay motivated when we face challenges?"

Victor replied, "Setbacks are a natural part of the journey toward success. Staying resilient and persistent is important, even when things get tough. Stay positive and remember why you set your goals in the first place. Seek feedback and support from your supervisors, mentors, and peers. And most importantly, don't give up."

Sameer nodded, "That makes sense. I'm excited to start setting and working towards achieving my goals."

Victor smiled, "I'm glad to hear that, Sameer. Setting career goals and preparing for the future is a lifelong journey. You can position yourself for success and achieve your dreams by staying focused, adaptable, and motivated."

As Victor finished speaking, he looked at the interns seated before him. Aarvi, Inaya, Druv, and Sameer had been eager to learn from him, and he was proud of their progress.

"I hope you found this final session helpful," Victor said. "Remember, setting career goals is not just about achieving success, but also about finding fulfillment in your work."

Aarvi nodded eagerly. " I'm excited to start setting my goals and working towards them."

"Me too," Inaya chimed in. "I realize now that I need to invest more in myself and my skills to achieve my goals."
Druv looked thoughtful. "I'm glad we talked about adaptability too. It's important to pivot and adjust when the corporate world changes."

Victor smiled, pleased with their responses. "Exactly. And remember, your goals can and should change over time as you grow and evolve. But having a plan will help you stay focused and motivated."

Sameer, who had been quiet for most of the session, spoke up. "I appreciate you taking the time to coach us, Mr. Victor. It means a lot."

Victor patted him on the back. "Of course, Sameer. That's what mentors are for. I want to see all of you succeed and reach your full potential."

The interns smiled gratefully at him, feeling inspired and ready to take on the world. With Victor's guidance and newfound knowledge, they knew they had the tools to prepare for the future and set meaningful career goals.

As they exited Victor's office, they turned back to see Victor standing by the table, looking into some papers. As they waved goodbye to him, he turned to them and said, "Well done, my young friends. You have accomplished much during your time here, and I do not doubt you will do great things in your future careers."

The interns thanked Victor for his guidance and support. He replied, "Remember, setting goals and preparing for the future is the key to success. And never forget the importance of hard work, dedication, and perseverance."

As they said their final goodbyes, the interns felt a sense of gratitude and appreciation for the opportunity to learn and grow under Victor's leadership. They knew they had been given a gift that would last a lifetime and were determined to make the most of it.

As the interns stepped out of the conference room, they couldn't help but feel a mix of emotions. Excitement for the future, sadness to leave their colleagues and mentors behind, and gratitude for the incredible opportunity they had been given.

Aarvi turned to Inaya, her eyes brimming with tears. "Can you believe it's over?" she asked, her voice barely above a whisper. "It feels like just yesterday we were walking through those doors for the first time."

Inaya nodded, a sad smile on her face. "I know. But we've come so far since then. We've learned so much and grown so much as individuals."

Druv put his arm around Sameer's shoulder. "And we couldn't have done it without each other," he said, a sense of camaraderie in his voice. "We're a team, and we'll always be there for each other, no matter where life takes us."

Sameer nodded, his eyes bright with determination. "And speaking of where life takes us," he said, a sly grin on his face, "I can't wait to see where we all end up. I have a feeling we're going to do amazing things."

Aarvi laughed, feeling a weight lift off her shoulders. "Yeah, me too. And who knows, maybe one day we'll all end up working together again."

As Aarvi, Inaya, Druv, and Sameer walked out of the elevator, they couldn't help but feel a sense of nostalgia. They knew the road ahead would be filled with challenges and obstacles, but they were ready to take them on, armed with the knowledge and skills they had gained during their internship.

As they walked out of the building, the sun shining bright overhead, they couldn't help but feel a sense of optimism for the future. They looked back at the towering skyscraper that housed the tech company where they had spent the past few months. They knew they would miss the vibrant energy and sense of community they had found there.

But as they turned their gaze toward the future, they felt a newfound sense of purpose. They had learned so much while at the company, not just about the tech industry, but about themselves. They had discovered their strengths and weaknesses, their passions and interests. They had formed bonds with their colleagues that they knew would last a lifetime.

And most importantly, they had been given the tools and guidance they needed to achieve their dreams. They had learned how to set goals, plan for the future, and stay motivated in the face of challenges. They knew the road ahead wouldn't be easy, but they were ready to face it head-on.

As they walked towards the cab, they exchanged knowing glances. They knew this was just the beginning of their journey and were excited to see where it would take them. They did not doubt that they would face obstacles and setbacks along the way, but they were ready to tackle them with the same determination and grit that had brought them this far.

As they stepped into the cab and headed back, they did so with pride and accomplishment. They had completed their internship but knew their journey was far from over. They were ready to take on the world, armed with the lessons they had learned and the memories they had made. They were ready to make their mark on the world, one step at a time.

*************** **THE END** ***************

About the Author

Sanath Nair is a seasoned sales and marketing professional with over 18 years of experience in the industry. With his B.Tech in Production Engineering and Master's in International Business, he has worked with some great teams and companies.

In his free time, he channels his creativity through writing and maintains a personal blog called Fresher Blog. He shares his thoughts and insights on various topics through his blog, showcasing his love for the written word.

https://fresherblog.com/